The Stages of Human Evolution: Human and Cultural Origins, *C. Loring Brace*

New World Prehistory: Archaeology of the American Indian, *William T. Sanders and Joseph J. Marino*

Culture Theory, *David Kaplan and Robert A. Manners*

Formation of the State, *Lawrence Krader*

Tribesmen, *Marshall D. Sahlins*

The Hunters, *Elman R. Service*

Peasants, *Eric R. Wolf*

FOUNDATIONS OF MODERN ANTHROPOLOGY SERIES

Marshall D. Sahlins, *Editor*

FOUNDATIONS OF MODERN ANTHROPOLOGY SERIES

PRENTICE-HALL, INC., *Englewood Cliffs, New Jersey*

William T. Sanders, The Pennsylvania State University

Joseph Marino, California State College

New World Prehistory

ARCHAEOLOGY OF THE AMERICAN INDIAN

© *Copyright 1970 by* PRENTICE-HALL, INC., *Englewood Cliffs, New Jersey*

All rights reserved. No part of this book may be reproduced

in any form by any means without permission

in writing from the publisher. Printed in the United States of America.

Library of Congress Catalog Card No. 70–98458.

Designed by Mark A. Binn

13–616185–5(p), 13–616193–6(c)

PRENTICE-HALL
FOUNDATIONS OF MODERN ANTHROPOLOGY SERIES

Marshall D. Sahlins, *Editor*

Current printing (last digit):
10   9   8   7   6   5   4

PRENTICE-HALL INTERNATIONAL, INC., *London*
PRENTICE-HALL OF AUSTRALIA, PTY., LTD., *Sydney*
PRENTICE-HALL OF CANADA, LTD., *Toronto*
PRENTICE-HALL OF INDIA, PVT. LTD., *New Delhi*
PRENTICE-HALL OF JAPAN, INC., *Tokyo*

Foundations

of Modern Anthropology

Series

The Foundations of Modern Anthropology Series is a documentation of the human condition, past and present. It is concerned mainly with exotic peoples, prehistoric times, unwritten languages, and unlikely customs. But this is merely the anthropologist's way of expressing his concern for the here and now, and his way makes a unique contribution to our knowledge of what's going on in the world. We cannot understand ourselves apart from an understanding of *man*, nor our culture apart from an understanding of *culture*. Inevitably we are impelled toward an intellectual encounter with man in all his varieties, no matter how primitive, how ancient, or how seemingly insignificant. Ever since their discovery by an expanding European civilization, primitive peoples have continued to hover over thoughtful men like ancestral ghosts, ever provoking this anthropological curiosity. To "return to the primitive" just for what it is would me foolish; the savage is not nature's nobleman and his existence is no halcyon idyll. For anthropology, the romance of the primitive has been something else: a search for the roots and meaning of ourselves—in the context of all mankind.

The series, then, is designed to display the varieties of man and culture and the evolution of man and culture. All fields of anthropology are relevant to the grand design and all of them—prehistoric archaeology, physical anthropology, linguistics, and ethnology (cultural anthropology)—are represented among the authors of the several books in the series. In the area of physical anthropology are books describing the early condition of humanity and the subhuman primate antecedents. The later development of man on the biological side is set out in the volume on races, while the archaeological accounts of the Old World and the New document development on the historical side. Then there are the studies of contemporary culture, including a book on how to understand it all—i.e., on ethnological theory—and one on language, the peculiar human gift responsible for it all. Main types of culture are laid out in "The Hunters," "Tribesmen," "Formation of the State," and "Peasants." Initiating a dialogue between contemplation of the primitive and the present, the volume on "The Present as Anthropology" keeps faith with the promise of anthropological study stated long ago by E. B. Tylor, who saw in it "the means of understanding our own lives and our place in the world, vaguely and imperfectly it is true, but at any rate more clearly than any former generation."

Contents

One   Introduction

There are perhaps as many definitions of cultural anthropology as there are anthropologists, but they all share the one central idea that what is involved is the scientific study of culture. A number of basic distinctions between culture and cultures, culture and cultural behavior, culture and parts of culture have been defined. Herskovits,[1] in summarizing some of these, has noted that cultures have both dynamic and static qualities, and that all functioning cultures are a balance of these two; that a particular culture may be described as an aggregate of specific characteristics, yet be characterized by a definite pattern or structure; that cultural behavior may be analyzed in terms of broad functional categories of behavior such as technology, economy, social organization, religion, language, and recreation—remembering always that these categories are functionally related and form an integrated whole in a particular culture; and finally, that although culture is a human universal, individual cultures are almost infinitely varied. Most anthropological research is an attempt to obtain generalizations about one or more of these basic principles. Perhaps the characteristic of culture that has most fascinated researchers is

---

[1] Melville J. Herskovits, *Man and His Works* (New York: Alfred A. Knopf, Inc., 1949), pp. 12–28.

that of variability. One influential consequence of the great voyages of discovery of the 16th century Europeans was to bring this phenomenon dramatically to the forefront of Western consciousness. A companion discovery was that culture is a universal shared by all mankind and that not only did all human groups have their own customs, but particular customs were to be found repeated in groups widely separated geographically; some customs were even to be found in all cultures. Not only were the broad cultural categories discerned universally, but more specific phenomena—including the nuclear family, suprafamily social organization, and belief in the soul (to cite a few examples)—were discovered in group after group.

Because cultural variations and similarities are clearly the product of historical forces, anthropologists seeking to explain them have been led to the study of cultural dynamics (the tendency of cultures to change in time) and statics (their tendency to resist change). A major research problem in seeking such explanations is methodological: How do we obtain our information for histories of specific cultures? Most anthropological methodology relies upon techniques of skilled observation of human behavior, together with methods of fairly direct interrogation of members of the society studied. But man's memory is short, and oral history, achieved through methods of direct observation and recording, rarely extends beyond three generations.

Historical documents have enriched the anthropologist's view of life in many parts of the ancient world, but even these have obvious deficiencies for the student seeking information on all aspects of culture. Aside from the limitations of subject matter of most written history, there is the fact that most cultures have been wholly nonliterate throughout their duration. Even literate cultures had at the outset enormously long nonliterate phases of development. In treating of the New World, of course, reliance upon historical texts is even less useful; most of man's development in this area has to be worked out by the anthropologist in the purely prehistoric dimension. The main methodological tools must therefore be those of archaeology.

Archaeology and Anthropology

This leads us to a brief discussion of the relationship between archaeology and anthropology. To many archaeologists, archaeology is an independent discipline; however, archaeology is here regarded as essentially a methodological system, since the phenomenon studied—man's cultural behavior—and the kinds of conclusions generated from archaeological data differ in no way from those of cultural anthropology generally.

The basic field techniques of archaeological research include surface survey and excavation. Surveys are conducted to locate and describe *sites*, here defined as any locality altered in some way by man in the past. Normally the first step in a program of archaeological research is to conduct a survey of the selected geographical unit. A site or sites may subsequently be selected for extensive or limited excavation to resolve specific problems or to amplify the picture of an ancient culture.

Analytically, archaeologists work on four levels. The first level is that of chronology, arrangement of artifacts and sites in sequences from earliest to latest. The second level may be characterized as an attempt to work out the ethnography of extinct cultures, that is, to provide as full a description as possible of all aspects of a vanished culture—first for a local geographical area, then for broader units. The third level involves a detailed comparison of the cultures of a defined geographical unit at different points in time to reconstruct a history of cultural development. The fourth and final level leads the archaeologist directly to those broad generalizations embracing cultural variation, statics, and dynamics that concern all cultural anthropologists, and it is at this level of generalization or theory that the archaeologist makes his most direct contribution to the broad field of cultural anthropology.

Tradition, Period, and Stage

A custom is the product of a continuing, standardized concensus of opinion about how an organized group of humans ought to perform a task. Like the term *culture, custom* has been used for both general and specific kinds of behavior. At times *custom* is used to describe brief segments in larger sequences of behavior, themselves called customs. We speak, for instance, of the Aztec custom of tying together the mantles worn by a couple in their wedding ceremony. Or we may speak of the custom of monogamous marriage. Even more broadly, we speak of general technological, economic, social, and religious customs.

Most archaeological evidence of customs involves technology, which can be analyzed with comparatively little difficulty on the basis of artifacts that archaeologists dig from the earth. Evidence of economic, social, and religious custom is usually indirect. Because the archaeologist must often work with material manifestations of customs and not with the customs themselves, and also because of a necessary preoccupation with cultural statics and dynamics or historical categories, he is more comfortable with the term *tradition*, which he substitutes for *custom*. Again, *tradition* may have a restricted, very specific meaning, as when we speak of a tradition of artistic representation of the human figure in a distinctive manner (in which case the term *style tradition* is frequently used); or the word may be employed in a broader sense, as in the expression "tradition of making and using pottery."

Indeed, *tradition* may be used when dealing with any general aspect of culture. One may speak of styles or traditions of government. The term may even serve in a more inclusive sense, as when we speak of a complete culture or a whole cultural tradition; for example, the buffalo-hunting tradition of the Plains Indians. Here we have reference to all of the economic, social, and religious ramifications of "buffalo-hunting" subsistence.

"Tradition" refers to a customary way of achieving a cultural objective, and in archaeology it always carries with it the connotation of duration in time. Specific stylistic traditions and whole cultural traditions may have awesome extensions in time. As we shall see, traditions also vary considerably in their horizontal or geographical distributions.

Period

Period refers to a major time segment in the culture of an area or region. We use this concept for the history of Western civilization when we organize it by centuries or millennia B.C. or A.D. However, most archaeologists and historians do not use such standardized blocks of time, but instead divide culture history into a series of segments of time, utilizing criteria of specific technological, political, or artistic style traditions—all of varying length, depending on duration of the style tradition selected. Minor changes within a style tradition divide periods into phases. Most culture history presents a continuing succession of gradual changes. The beginnings or endings of so-called periods do not represent sudden abandonments or initiations of style traditions. For this reason, periods have conventionally been defined from artifacts characteristic of the middle of the period. Sudden shifts of style traditions are normally products of intensified contact with neighboring geographical units possessing distinctive stylistic histories. When a stylistic tradition that has evolved in one geographical unit spreads over a larger region, replacing local styles, the term *horizon style* is frequently used. Horizon styles are useful in establishing *synchronisms*, that is, the cross dating of local culture histories.

Period divisions based on stylistic traditions, with the exception of horizon styles, are readily defined only for relatively small geographical units. When larger units are involved we find that space, like time, appears to promote stylistic differentiation. It is for this reason that archaeologists, in summarizing continental culture histories, customarily turn to the concept of the *culture area*. Although the culture or society of each organized group of humans is always different in detail from that of every other group, large numbers of societies that share boundaries share cultural characteristics. Culture areas are defined by anthropologists on the basis of the common possession, among groups, of traits of a more generalized nature than those implied by style traditions. For example, tribes such as the Cheyenne, Teton-Dakota, and Crow, in the grassy plains of the American West in the 19th century, were all characterized by a subsistence based on buffalo hunting, lived in skin tepees, were periodically organized into large hunting bands, and participated in the Sun Dance, to name a few of their commonly held traits. This similarity in culture was quite obviously the product of similar or related historical processes. For this reason, the culture area is capable of providing a useful as well as convenient geographical unit for the analysis of culture history. The complex of traits that is used in the definition of culture areas forms a tradition of the type that we have referred to as a whole culture tradition.

One major problem in periodization of the history of these large areas is that of the relative precocity and retardation between the smaller geographical subunits. It is usual to select one of the more precocious areas and define periods on the basis of the local history of that area. We may note as example the device adopted for Mesoamerica, where in one local stylistic region, that of the Lowland Maya, stone stelae inscribed with dates were erected between 300 and 900 A.D. in a nearly unbroken sequence. This time segment is known to researchers as the Classic Period, and all contemporary local cultures in the Mesoamerican culture area are referred to as Classic cultures, whether they erected stelae or even possessed writing. The period following this and lasting up to the Spanish Conquest is therefore called the Postclassic. It can be seen that the terms Classic and Postclassic when so used have a purely chronological connotation.

The term *stage* denotes a temporal segment of culture history characterized by the appearance of selected cultural traits and complexes. Most chronological charts for culture areas, divided by periods, show a series of parallel vertical columns representing geographical subdivisions with separate style histories, together with a series of horizontal lines running across the chart for period beginnings and endings. In a chart showing stages, the horizontal lines, as we follow them across the page, form a series of steps, the height of which reflects precocity or retardation of specific areas as defined by appearance or lack of the characteristics used to define stages. In some subareas, a particular stage may not even appear.

Most stage definitions have been based on technological changes, primarily because direct data used for archaeological formulations are technological. The well-known Old World sequence of Paleolithic, Neolithic, Chalcolithic, Bronze, and Iron Ages is possibly the most familiar example. These stages imply no universal chronology. The date of inception of each stage varied considerably from geographical subarea to subarea. For example, the Bronze Age began at about 3000 b.c. in Mesopotamia, but did not begin until 1500 b.c. in Scandinavia. For reasons to be presented in the following sections, we should prefer to employ a stage system based on nontechnological criteria. Such a system has been designed by Service[2] and will be utilized in this book with some modification. The basic assumption of his scheme is that the infinite variety of societies described by anthropologists can be divided and grouped into a series of five broad types based on organization or structure. These types will be here referred to as bands, tribes, chiefdoms, ancient states, and industrial states. The first four types, which are the concern of the New World prehistorian, are defined as follows:

1. *Bands.* These are small societies, usually numbering less than one hundred people, that possess a common territory and are characterized by local exogamy. Bands are the simplest societies known, loosely integrated by limited "conceptions of kinship extended by marriage alliances."[3] Service hypothesizes that before contact with Western civilization all bands were virilocal and that each band tended to consist of related men, their foreign wives (i.e. from other bands), and their unmarried children. Bands characteristically are hunters and gatherers who shift residence seasonally as plant food resources become depleted or in response to seasonal changes in location of game. Bands lack formal leaders, and economic or political rank differences between individuals are almost nonexistent. Bands are therefore integrated primarily by kin obligations and ties. Subsistence resources are normally communally owned, and there is almost no occupational and community specialization, although some trade between bands is usually present as the product of uneven distribution of resources. Trade, however, is neither extensive nor intensive, and special institutions are lacking. The only social differentiation within the band is determined by age and sex.

---

[2] Elman R. Service, *Primitive Social Organization* (New York: Random House, Inc., 1962), pp. 60–177.

[3] Elman R. Service, *The Hunters* (Englewood Cliffs, N.J.: Prentice-Hall, Inc., 1966), p. 7.

2. *Tribes.* Although they are larger societies than bands, tribes rarely exceed more than a few thousand members. They are generally found among farmers, and their members live in relatively or completely permanent settlements. Such settlements may be tightly nucleated, in which case we can call them *villages,* or settlement may be dispersed, in which case the term *neighborhood* is preferable. Individual settlements are frequently of the size of bands, but usually they are larger, and in a few cases entire tribes live in villages of several thousand inhabitants. Normally, tribes are multicommunity societies. Individual communities are integrated into the larger society by theoretical descent groups or *sibs,* usually based on the unilineal principle, and by voluntary associations (warriors clubs, religious fraternities, age-grades, and sets), memberships of which intersect the local communities. Tribes are composed of individual communities frequently made up of one or more true descent groups or lineages, and hence are primitive segmentary societies.[4] Some are relatively amorphous bodies where the communities are integrated solely by intermarriage, kinship ties, non-aggression pacts, and by the sharing of a common culture, language, territory, and name. In other tribes, sibs or associations have internal hierarchies of officials, hold periodic meetings and ceremonies to renew and strengthen their ties, and possess political and religious functions. More thoroughly organized tribes may have a "capital," or village seat of government, and a hierarchy of tribal leaders. Even in these cases, officials of a tribal society lack the economic base necessary for effective exercise of power, and ranking —either within or between communities—is lacking. Economic institutions in tribes are relatively simple. Trade may be extensive, but it is not so intensive as to require markets or full-time occupational specialists.

3. *Chiefdoms.* It is with chiefdoms that a new structural principle for integration of multicommunity societies appears: ranking. In chiefdoms, lineages are graded on a prestige ladder, and it is not uncommon for one of the lineages to reserve right of tenure for the political office that Service refers to as *chief.* Frequently present is the concept that all members share common descent from a single ancestor, and that ranking of lineages and individuals will be based on a principle of primogeniture. Everyone in this scheme is related to the chief, and everyone also occupies a unique position of rank that is determined by calculation of the exact degree of closeness (or distance) to the chief. A result is that true stratification into classes is absent, as there are no large groups made up of people of equivalent rank. The society is still based on kinship, with ranking mechanisms added as new structural principles. In such societies, the person of the chief is almost sacrosanct, and he frequently plays a vital sacerdotal role. He is surrounded by a retinue of wives, retainers, and assistants, and contact with him is restricted and patterned by elaborate rules of protocol. His life crises of birth, marriage, and—most particularly—death are frequently accompanied by elaborate public ritual. Service refers to the prescriptions for these ceremonial practices as *sumptuary rules.*

The chief's primary economic basis of power lies in his role as a redistributor of goods. In chiefdom societies, local specialization in craft

---

[4] Service, *Primitive Social Organization.*

products and in production of foodstuffs and raw materials is highly developed. Characteristically, surpluses of these goods are periodically produced by local kin groups and paid as kin obligations to the chief. He in turn uses these surpluses for maintenance of his court and, more importantly, for redistribution to his subjects. Chiefs in these systems can also command periodic contributions of labor for construction and maintenance of their houses or courts, and of other public buildings, such as temples. These contributions are symbolically rationalized as kin obligations and involve reciprocal payment by the chief in the form of goods, particularly food. The chief derives his power from the sumptuary and redistributive practices noted above. Markets are generally absent or weakly developed, and full-time craft specialization is limited to artisans attached to the chiefly household.

The settlement pattern of chiefdoms may vary considerably and include local kin-based communities of both village and neighborhood type. One new settlement type appears, however, that clearly distinguishes a chiefdom from a tribe: the center or capital. Here are situated temples, the chief's residence, and the houses of his servants; here dwell craftsmen, political assistants, priests and craftsmen. The population of a center of this kind in a large chiefdom can run into thousands. Most higher-ranking officials are usually close kinsmen of the chief, and his entire lineage would normally reside there. In times and places where the prevailing social atmosphere is one of intense warfare, all or most of the population may be nucleated at the center, forming an unusually large settlement. Chiefdoms as a whole are larger societies than tribes, but there is considerable overlap in size. The mode is probably between 5000 and 20,000, but Polynesian chiefdoms ranging from less than 1000 to 100,000 are known. Very small chiefdoms are, however, characterized by a great reduction of prestige in the chiefly position and very large ones are usually short-lived extensions of power by unusually able individual chiefs of great charismatic force.

4. *Ancient States.* Many of the principles obtaining in chiefdoms—sumptuary rules, ranking systems, the dichotomy between center and dependent settlements, and the leader as dispenser of gifts and general goods —serve in the organization of ancient states. However, there are a number of important differences. Most ancient states were quite highly centralized, with power concentrated in the hands of a single leader. The leader's position, like that of a chief, was limited to a ruling lineage. The entire society, however, is not rationalized as a great kin group, but rather is viewed as a territory owned by the ruling lineage and populated by tenants or peasants. The relationship between owner and tenant is that of a legal contract involving mutual rights, obligations, duties, and privileges. Frequently, the relationship is rationalized ideologically by a myth of divine descent for the ruler and his lineage.

The ruler, or *king* as we shall refer to him, has the explicit authority to establish laws and to enforce them through a standing army, police force, and court system, all of which are lacking in chiefdoms; he administers his estate through a bureaucracy of appointed officials. Although chiefs can command services and collect surpluses from their subjects, these are considered as kin contributions, and we note a heavy ideological focus on reciprocation. Though the contractual relationship between king and subject has strong reciprocal qualities, the balance of payment is much more unevenly weighted in favor of the ruler than that seen in chiefdoms. Furthermore, the contributions are explicitly recognized as rents or taxes.

The king may retain certain sacerdotal functions like those of the chief, but most of these are performed by members of a large, semi-autonomous institution that we can call the *temple*. The king may also retain certain redistributive functions, but the larger part of these are performed by professional merchants through the institution known as the *market*.

Eric Wolf has noted that "the rulers have commonly settled in special centers" [5] that may or may not be urban. The distinction between urban and nonurban centers should be emphasized. In the nonurban type, the center is comparable in function, and to some degree in structure, to chiefdom centers. The center of a nonurban state is essentially a huge, extended royal household composed of residences of the royal lineage, bureaucrats, priests, royal craftsmen, and soldiers. At the heart of such centers are government buildings, temples, and markets. Such centers differ from those of chiefdoms in their greater size and internal complexity. The expression *ceremonial center* is frequently used for this type of settlement.

Urban states, in contrast, are characterized by a settlement-type referred to as a *town* (associated with small states) or *city* (associated with large states). In urban centers, whether towns or cities, are found large nucleated aggregations of dwellings and evidences of considerably greater economic and social differentiation than is present in centers of nonurban states or chiefdoms. Particularly characteristic of such centers are great numbers of craft specialists who are not attached to royal or noble households, but who produce goods for the market and live within a market economy. In ancient states, because of limitations of the production technologies utilized, many of these specialists work as such for only part of the time, practicing some agriculture outside the city or town. There is a tendency to limit full-time specialization to practitioners of the elite crafts. Owing to the partial dependence of most cities in ancient urban states on a system of agriculture that had to be managed with rather primitive tools, such states have for the most part evolved only under those very special environmental conditions that permitted support of highly productive farming systems.

Ancient states, urban and nonurban alike, vary considerably in size. Their populations generally run into the scores of thousands, and the maximum is probably best represented by the Roman Empire, with its estimated 50,000,-000 inhabitants. In culture areas where states have great historical depth and have become traditional forms, even smaller populations may be organized on this basis. In any event, the population mode and maximum far exceed those of chiefdoms.

Identification of Prehistoric Stages

A major problem in utilizing the types presented by Service is methodological. How do we identify them in an archaeological or pre-

[5] Eric R. Wolf, *Peasants* (Englewood Cliffs, N.J.: Prentice-Hall, Inc., 1966), p. 10.

historic context? The major differences between them lie in societal size and degree of internal differentiation. Those criteria that relate to these two features seem to be found most readily in studies of *whole settlement patterns* and in classification of sites and architectural units to be found within these patterns. The size, plan, and quality of houses within a community reflect differences in social status, and, more specifically, artifacts found within a house may identify the nature of the statuses of the householders. Excavations and surveys of houses from entire sites permit evaluation of degree of rank and occupational differentiation found in the ancient community; they also provide at least a rough estimate of population.

Aside from evidence of internal differentiation within sites, community stratification provides critical clues to the size and internal complexity of the entire society. By *community stratification* is meant all those obvious and clear cases of differences in quality of houses as a whole, together with the amount and degree of monumentality of public architecture from one site to the next. Other clues can be obtained from pictorial art, quality of artifacts, evidence of trade, or in evidence of mass production, or manufacture.

In the archaeological record of settlement pattern, bands and tribes may be easily set off from chiefdoms and states by lack of evidence of societal differentiation *within* sites, or of ranking *between* sites. Bands are so closely related to a hunting and gathering subsistence, and the latter, in turn, to seasonal movement of residence, that most band sites are easily identifiable.

Most food-producers, if not members of a chiefdom or a state, are tribally organized. A band-like structure might occur among farmers living in a very inhospitable environment with small, widely spaced settlements. In this study, we will generally assume that groups with a hunting and gathering subsistence base had a band organization and that farming cultures without evidence of ranking were tribally organized.

The most difficult problem of identification lies in the attempt to separate chiefdoms from states, particularly from nonurban states, since in all cases urban centers should be readily identified. Differences between chiefdoms and states are as much quantitative as they are qualitative. Our major criteria here will be found in the number of levels of community stratification and in the size, quality, and complexity of function and plan of the public architectural complexes of the largest centers known for a period and an area.

Another possible guide lies in funerary customs. If sumptuary rites are of special significance in chiefdoms, then theoretically the archaeological remains should show an unusual emphasis on burial ritual. However, great care must be exercised in using this criterion, since sumptuary rites also characterize states; furthermore, ancestral cults may be highly elaborated even among large, complex states. In utilizing this criterion, therefore, the archaeologist must make speculative estimates of the relative amount of surplus energy devoted by a prehistoric population to the funerary rites of chiefs, in contrast to the construction and maintenance of the temples and palaces of kings.

Theoretical Considerations

With a few notable exceptions, historians tend to stress the individuality or uniqueness of each stylistic or cultural tradition, while largely eschewing generalizations about culture change as a whole. The counterpart of this approach in anthropology is seen in the dominance of analyses of the culture histories of individual culture areas.

Viewed in detail, culture area histories are unique indeed; they are all products of a process called *diffusion*. This term refers to the process by which a cultural innovation spreads from its source, and to the steps by which it becomes integrated into a cultural system. When most archaeologists refer to diffusion they have in mind the spread of customs from one society to another. Here the definition is broadened to include the process by which innovations become accepted as customs by the society of the innovator as well.

Diffusion within culture areas is intensive and extensive, in part because of the varying relative facility of contact; groups situated close to each other geographically have greater opportunities to imitate customs than groups widely spaced. The second reason diffusion occurs readily within culture areas is a more critical one. Most of culture (in fact all of it, if one takes a broad view) has developed as an adaptation to environment. Environment is here taken as both natural and social. Both types of environments operate on innovations in a selective way; therefore, innovations that become customs are clearly those that were well-adapted, and other groups residing in the same social and geographical environment are likely to adopt them because they were successful.

Not all innovations are equally adaptive. With respect to adaptation to the natural environment, Steward [6] has defined what he calls the *culture core*, those aspects of a culture that have strong adaptive value. Subsistence systems are particularly significant parts of this core.

One of the most fruitless arguments in the history of anthropology has been over the relative significance of innovation (or invention) and diffusion as factors of cultural change. Innovations are made either by accident or intentionally by individuals of unusual talent. There is no evidence that either occurs more commonly in one human population than another. Isolated human societies would be expectedly less dynamic than entire culture areas. The difference in part is simply demographic; the larger the population, the higher the odds are the innovations will occur. Furthermore, the relatively high facility of communication between groups residing in the same culture area means that the diffusion of an innovation is likely to occur before its reinvention.

Diffusion may occur by a variety of mechanisms; migration, intermarriage, warfare, trade, social visiting, and religious conversion are all important means by which innovations diffuse.

An important distinction is that drawn by Roland Dixon [7] between

[6] Julian H. Steward, *Theory of Culture Change* (Urbana, Ill.: University of Illinois Press, 1955).
[7] Roland B. Dixon, *The Building of Cultures* (New York: Charles Scribner's Sons, 1923).

Primary Diffusion (diffusion within a culture area) and Secondary Diffusion (between culture areas). Secondary Diffusion is undoubtedly a less common event. Both the distance between culture areas and the fact that innovations useful in one geographical region are frequently not adaptable to others would act to reduce the probability of Secondary Diffusion.

We have stressed the uniqueness of the history of each culture area and of each geographic environment and suggested that the interaction between man and the natural environment was a powerful force in the evolution of cultures. On the other hand, geographers classify environments into types. Even granting that a variety of adaptive responses are possible to a given environmental type, the number of responses is nevertheless limited and, in part at least, strikingly different from those possible in another type of environment. This means that the history of culture areas with similar environments should show marked parallelisms. This view has been developed by Julian Steward,[8] who refers to the process as *multilineal evolution*. He uses as an example a series of culture areas characterized by arid to subhumid tropical environments—the Near East, Egypt, North China, Mesoamerica, and the Central Andes—and demonstrates striking parallelisms in their historical development.

Other anthropologists have carried this taxonomic device one step further and considered all of human cultural development as proceeding along a single main line of development. This line leads from small societies to large ones, from simply structured to complexly structured societies, from simple tools to more efficient tools, from a relatively slight utilization of resources to an increasingly fuller use, and from a low energy output per capita to a high one. This process, referred to as *unilineal evolution*, is usually visualized as the product of a series of technological steps improving the energy output of man and consequently requiring new means of social, economic, and religious organization. As an overall assessment of human development it is undoubtedly a correct picture, but the postulated technological revolutions are few in number (they resolve themselves into three: Tool-Making, Food-Producing, and Fuel), thus providing us with a very broad picture of human history and of course leaving unexplained the entire matter of precocity and retardation—why stages appear earlier in one region than in another. In some regions the food-producing revolution led to cities and empires, in others to tribes.

We will utilize a combination of these various principles of cultural dynamics in our analysis of New World culture history. Service's Band–Tribe–Chiefdom–Ancient State–Industrial State stages provide a somewhat more sophisticated theory of unilineal evolution than that based solely on technological stages, and we will use it in the basic organization of this book, testing it against the data from New World archaeology. The concept of multilineal evolution will provide a useful tool for attacking the question of precocity and retardation between and within culture areas, and the concepts of diffusion and specific environmental adaptation will provide the theoretical framework for the brief summaries of culture area histories.

---

[8] Steward, *Theory of Culture Change.*

Two The New World as a Theater of Cultural History

For anthropologists interested in cultural variation and the historical forces that shape it, the New World is an extraordinarily productive area of research. At the time of Columbus the variation in language and culture over this huge double continent was truly extraordinary. In this chapter we shall briefly summarize this variation and indicate those major problems of its culture history that have most concerned anthropologists.[1]

Geography, Past and Present

The New World can be thought of as one huge continental island extending from the Arctic to the Antarctic. The equator bisects the island producing the phenomenon of comparable climatic zones to the north and

---

[1] The following general works provide a useful introduction to the culture areas of the New World. Harold E. Driver, *Indians of North America* (Chicago: University of Chicago Press, 1961); Robert F. Spencer *et al.*, *The Native Americans* (New York: Harper and Row, Publishers, Inc., 1965); Julian H. Steward and Louis C. Faron, *Native Peoples of South America* (New York: McGraw-Hill Book Company, 1959).

south. Only in the extreme northwest does the coastline closely approach that of the Old World land mass.

An almost continuous range of young, rugged mountains runs down the western side of the double continent from Alaska to Tierra del Fuego. The narrow center (Middle America) is almost filled by them; north and south of Middle America are two huge lowland plains, one in each continent and each drained by enormous river basins. The Pacific Coastal Plain that borders the ranges is everywhere narrow and in places nonexistent. Older, lower, and gentler ranges parallel the Atlantic coast in North and South America. With notable exceptions, rains from the Pacific side are light, and the Pacific Coastal Plain, escarpment, interior valleys, and basins tend to be dry; rains from the Atlantic, in contrast, are more abundant and dependable.

With respect to human occupation a useful broad classification of New World environments is that proposed by Preston James.[2] It includes the following types: polar; boreal forest; mixed latitude forest; grassland, with variants based on temperature and rainfall; tropical forest; dry lands; and Mediterranean scrub forests.

The polar type is an Arctic desert, with long, cold winters and short, cool summers. Agriculture is impossible and wild food resources thin. Plant foods are virtually nonexistent for most of the year and inland hunting is poor. The major food resource is found in sea mammals. This type is restricted to the Canadian and Alaskan Arctic and to the North Pacific coasts and offshore islands.

Immediately south and occupying most of Canada is a belt of boreal forest. The climate is humid and characterized by long, cold winters, with heavy snowfall, and short, hot summers. The summer season is too brief for any agriculture that involves native crops. Vegetation useful as food for man is poor. Fauna is varied, with numerous large species (bear, elk, moose, deer), but thinly dispersed; it is nonmigratory and lives in family groups or small herds. The Pacific littoral segment of the region has a mountainous, complexly indented coastline with numerous offshore islands. It is one of the world's richest fishing grounds; particularly abundant are herring, halibut, smelt, euchelon, and salmon. Another boreal littoral region is found on the south coast of Chile, but it lacks the abundant fishing resources of the Canadian coast. The major food resource there is shellfish.

South of the U.S.–Canadian border the temperature regime is favorable for aboriginal agriculture. Characteristic of the United States as a whole are sharp seasonal extremes of temperature with cold winters and hot summers. These extremes are greatest in the northern part of the country; winters become much milder in the south. Generally there is a high-to-low gradient of rainfall from east to west. The eastern half of the country was covered by a vast forest of the type called by James a *mid-latitude mixed forest* and consisting of a combination of deciduous hardwoods and conifers. Wild plant food resources are much more abundant than in the northern forests; particularly significant are nut-bearing trees: hickory and oak. Fauna

---

[2] Preston E. James, *An Outline of Geography* (Boston, Mass.: Ginn and Company, 1935).

here is as varied as, or more varied than, it is in the north; it is also of much higher density, and generally consists of varieties of the same basic species or genera. Soils are extremely variable in quality with respect to agricultural use; the best lands are the alluvial plains of major rivers.

Moving westward, rainfall decreases and vegetation shifts through a series of grassland types. This huge stretch of mid-latitude grassland was one of the world's richest hunting grounds. Vast herds of migratory game, particularly bison, roamed the rolling plains at the time of European contact. Soils are deep, black, and exceptionally good for modern plow agriculture, but the dense sod formed by the roots of native grasses limited aboriginal cultivation to the narrow gallery forests on the flood plains of the major rivers. A comparable region south of the equator includes most of Argentina but with much poorer useful fauna—primarily guanaco and rhea.

A tropical counterpart of the temperate grasslands, frequently referred to as savanna by geographers, occupies most of eastern Brazil, the Gran Chaco, and a nearly continuous strip through eastern Colombia, southern Venezuela, and interior Guyana. Small areas of savanna are also found within regions of the tropical forest, the product either of poor drainage or of poor soils. Hunting resources, as in the Argentine grasslands, are surprisingly poor. Richer food resources are found in the rivers where alligators, turtle, tapir, and fish are available. Wild plant foods are relatively abundant, particularly in the Chaco, and include wild rice, algarroba pods, pine nuts, and palm fruits. Agriculture in the South American grasslands in aboriginal times seems to have been limited to gallery forests even though tropical grasses are generally not sod-forming.

Most of the vast drainage basin of the Amazon-Orinoco system is covered by tropical forests. Distinctive features include heavy rainfall, slight seasonal variations in temperature, a twelve-month growing season, and abundant surface drainage. The vigorous vegetation and generally poor soils (the product of a process called *leaching*) have kept the region culturally and demographically marginal. The better lands are found in the alluvial plains and in the hilly terrain, where leaching is reduced by more rapid runoff. Conditions are also more favorable in areas where annual rainfall is below 2000 mm and has a strongly seasonal distribution. For most of the basin, wild plant and animal foods are considerably poorer (except in the rivers) than in adjacent savannas.

In central Chile and California a special environmental type played a very minor role in New World culture history, in sharp contrast to its counterpart in the Old World, the Mediterranean scrub forest; it is a subtropical type with dry, hot summers and rainy, cool winters. The annual rainfall is between 200 and 1000 mm. The vegetation is predominantly a scrub oak–conifer forest. Wild plant resources are extraordinarily rich in this type, richest in this respect in the world. Particularly important are acorns and wild grasses. The marginal historical role of this type in New World history derives from the small size of the two regions described and the fact that New World crops were tropical in origin and poorly adapted to the frosty winters.

Dry lands occupy much of the western third of the United States and adjacent northern Mexico. Most of this region is also mountainous and consists of plateaus, valleys and basins; temperature and soil conditions are excellent for agriculture. Here, the major problem is water. Drylands also vary considerably in wild food resources, depending on variation in total annual rainfall and its seasonal distribution. In mountainous dry lands there is usually heavier precipitation on slopes, and these provide runoff water for plant growth lower down. Wild grasses and beans, roots and fruit of xerophytic plants may be relatively abundant.

James's low-latitude mountain environment is a critical one for New World culture history. This is a tropical type in which the land form is dominated by mountains. Variation in elevation above sea level, direction of ranges, and relationship to monsoon winds all produce an extraordinary, diversified environment with almost all the environmental types described above occurring in close juxtaposition. This type is generally characteristic of the mountainous backbone of the continent between central Mexico and Bolivia.

Most human physical and cultural evolution has taken place during the final million years or so of the history of the earth, a period referred to by geologists as the Pleistocene Epoch. During this long epoch there was an extension of Arctic glaciers over enormous territories; this occurred at least four, and probably five, times. There was also a parallel extension of mountain glaciers downslope. These epochs are referred to as glacials; they caused striking changes in temperature, precipitation, and, as a consequence, in flora and fauna over huge continental regions. Periods in between are referred to as interglacials and are characterized by a return to warmer conditions. Since man evolved in the Old World and apparently did not enter the New World earlier than the Third Interglacial, we need not concern ourselves here with the early ice advances and retreats. But the subject of Pleistocene geology has relevance for three reasons. First, and on a methodological level, the association of archaeological artifacts with older and buried geological strata formed during the Pleistocene is an aid to dating them. More importantly, the fourth glacial advance (called *Wisconsin* in North America) and the immediate post-Pleistocene period brought striking changes in environment to huge areas of the New World. Thus adaptation has not been a static process, but an everchanging one. Finally, the distribution of ice—particularly in the north—is a critical factor in understanding population movements into and within the New World.

During the Wisconsin Glacial Advance the climatic zones of North America shifted to the south. Much of the northeastern portion of the United States was occupied by conifer forests comparable to the Canadian boreal forest of today; the southeastern part of the United States was then more like the contemporary Northeast in climate and vegetation. As the ice advanced, it brought moisture, making of the northern plains a lush tundra or Arctic grassland; the dry lands of the Southwest were transformed into either succulent deserts or shortgrass grasslands. During interstadials the climate was both warmer and drier. After the final retreat of the ice, there was a short minor glaciation around 6000 B.C., followed by a gradual return to the warmer and drier conditions characteristic of today.

In Middle and South America glacial advances had much less striking effects. Glaciers moved downslope only a few hundred meters from their present position in the mountains. They did, however, bring moister conditions to lower-lying areas; the present coastal deserts of Peru and Chile are essentially the product of the post-Pleistocene glacial recession.

Linguistic Diversity

Linguists have estimated that in 1492 there were between 2000 and 2200 languages spoken in the New World, each at least as distant in vocabulary and grammar from the other as English is from German. Nearly all European languages, with notable exceptions, show close resemblances in root words, and linguists group them into what is known as a language family or linguistic stock. These resemblances are of considerable historical significance since they indicate a common origin in the past followed by subsequent differentiation. The latter is the product of historical forces that tend to isolate, particularly population movements or migrations. Cultures of migrating groups tend to change drastically and rapidly as they adapt to new natural and social environments, but languages are much more resistant to change. Analysis of language relationships in the New World therefore provides clues to prehistoric population movements.

Around the turn of the century, a concerned effort was made to organize American Indian languages into stocks. Approximately 130 were suggested for the New World. Subsequent research resulted in transfer of some languages from smaller to larger stocks, effecting a reduction in number. More recent studies have proposed the grouping of a number of stocks into phyla and superphyla that represent much older phases of differentiation.

Swadesh has defined five superphyla: Macro-Carib, Macro-Arawakan, Macro-Quechuan, Macro-Mayan, and Bask-Dennean (which includes some Asian languages). He suggests that each represents a separate migration into the New World, and that they arrived in the order given.[3] Greenberg would group Macro-Arawak with Macro-Quechuan, assigning both to an Andean-Equatorial superphylum.[4]

Following Spencer and Jennings for North and Middle America and Steward and Faron (who use the Greenberg system) for South America, distribution of phyla and superphyla is as follows.[5] The Bask Dennean superphylum was found primarily in northwestern North America and includes three phyla, Eskaleut, Na-Dene, and Mosan.

The Macro-Maya superphylum includes most of the languages of North and Middle America and includes the following phyla: Aztec-Tanoan, Penutian, Totonac-Mayan, Macro-Otomangean, Algonkin, Hokan-Coahuiltecan, and Chibchan. The Aztec-Tanoan phylum was distributed within a territory that included the Great Basin and the southwestern portion of the United States, most of northern Mexico, and the Central Mexican

[3] Morris H. Swadesh, "Linguistic Overview," in Jesse D. Jennings and Edward Norbeck, *Prehistoric Man in the New World* (Chicago: University of Chicago Press, 1963), pp. 527–528.

[4] Joseph H. Greenberg, "The General Classification of Central and South American Languages," in *Men and Cultures*, A.F.C. Wallace, ed., Selected Papers, 5th International Congress of Anthropological and Ethnological Sciences (Philadelphia: University of Pennsylvania Press, 1964), pp. 741–794.

[5] Steward and Faron, *Native Peoples of South America*, pp. 16–30.

Plateau, with outliers scattered throughout southern Middle America. The Penutian was found primarily on the coast and in interior valleys of the Pacific watershed of the United States, Totonac-Mayan in southern and eastern Mexico and Guatemala. These three have been grouped by some linguists into a larger taxonomic level between the superphylum and phylum.

Algonkin speakers are usually considered as a separate phylum and were found primarily in the northeastern part of the United States and in eastern Canada. Other linguists have placed them within a huge, widespread, internally complex superphylum that includes at least seven linguistic stocks: Hokan, Coahuiltecan, Siouan-Yuchi, Iroquoian, Caddoan, Gulf, and Subtiaba-Tlapanec. Excluding Algonkin, languages of this group prevailed in most of the central and eastern portions of the United States in 1492 and had scattered outliers (Tlapanec, Subtiaba, Jicaque) in Mexico, Nicaragua, Honduras, and even on the Pacific coast of Colombia.

Macro-Otomangean was found entirely in central and southern Mexico. Chibchan is the only phylum that is well represented on both continents, taking in most of Central America east of Guatemala, nearly all of Colombia, and with outliers on the coasts of Ecuador, Peru, and Chile and in scattered localities in the Orinoco and Amazon drainages.

Macro-Carib was found primarily in the Gran Chaco, Eastern Brazil, the eastern foothills of the Andes, and interior Guyana in 1492. Steward's and Faron's Andean-Equatorial superphylum occupied the balance of South America. The Andean phylum or the Macro-Quechuan superphylum of Swadesh was found essentially in highland Ecuador, Peru, Bolivia, most of Chile and Argentina, and on most of the Peruvian coast. The Equatorial phylum, on the other hand, was distributed along the major rivers and tributaries of the Orinoco, Amazon, and La Plata drainages, with an extension into the West Indies.

We will return to the taxonomy of New World languages at several points in our narrative in connection with problems of population movement.

Cultural Diversity: Bands

In 1492, bands were found primarily in Canada, Alaska, the western third of the United States, and the southern third of South America.

All groups in these regions shared certain basic cultural features. All were hunters and gatherers, used a variety of wood, stone, bone, or ivory tools, lacked metallurgy, and relied heavily on containers fashioned of skin or basketry in preference to pottery. All used relatively simple portable houses and shifted residence frequently, at least part of the year. The groups differed strikingly in kinds of wild resources emphasized and, therefore, the specific tools used, the quantity and quality of clothing, the presence and absence of more substantial houses, and the degree to which extended seasonal residence on single sites was feasible. All these variations relate specifically to variations of the natural environment.

Socially, all were organized in nuclear or extended families, and this was the most important social group; in some societies it was the only stable functioning social group. In most cases, however, nuclear families gathered seasonally into bands. There was considerable variation in size, permanence of residence and membership, rule of residence, and function and structure of the band; variation dependent primarily on abundance and character of food resources. Maximum size of such bands, however, was perhaps several hundred persons, and most were of fewer than 100. All groups either lacked entirely, or showed slight development of, formal power systems, warfare, ranking or social stratification, trade, theoretical descent groups, and economic specialization.

Religion was focused primarily on life crisis rites, ceremonies to increase or to ensure the food supply, and curing ceremonies. The only specialized profession was the part-time shaman.

Writers disagree on the precise number of culture areas definable in the New World in 1492. We shall favor a grouping of regions occupied by *bands* into six major culture areas, three in each continent. The generalizations made above apply to all, and below we have briefly summarized a few special characteristics found in each area.

1. Arctic Hunters

Survival in this extreme environment requires a highly specialized adaptation, first to the cold, secondly to the means necessary to obtain food. The historic Eskimo utilized tailored fur garments; he dwelt in substantial houses of sod, ice, bone, and driftwood during the cold winters, and these he equipped with fur insulation, oil lamps, and storm entrances. During summers he lived in portable skin tents. A key to subsistence in the area is effective transportation; thus, skin boats were used in summer and dog sleds in winter. Primary foods were sea mammals; the main hunting tool was the harpoon; the technology heavily emphasized ivory and bone. Eskimo society was characterized by loose band membership and weak territoriality, the product of erratic and thinly spread food resource.

2. Northern Forest Hunters

Bands in the interior of Canada represent adaptation to a boreal forest. Population was extremely scanty, the result of poor food resources. Some technology paralleled that of the Eskimo: substantial winter houses, (in this area of logs); portable summer houses of bark; use of dog toboggans and snowshoes in winter, of bark canoes in summer; and tailored garments. Land hunting was the major food source and included as techniques trapping and stalking with bows; chipped and ground stone tools were characteristic. Socially, bands split into two types differing primarily in terms of summer activities. Both types wintered in macroband camp sites. Those that hunted entirely within the forest divided into family units for summer hunting. Others followed migratory caribou into the tundra in large cooperative bands under hunting headmen.

3. The Western Food-gatherers

We have grouped the huge area that includes the western third of the United States into a single culture area characterized by heavy dependence on wild plant foods, particularly seeds, for subsistence. Most writers have divided it into three or four culture areas: California, the Plateau, the Great Basin, and the Southwest, but much of the variation in culture is the product of variations in quantity of the same basic foods. In central California, acorns and wild grasses were so abundant that bands became completely sedentary; foraging expeditions from the central camps were of short duration and involved families or individuals, not the entire band. However, even the largest Californian bands numbered only a few hundred members. With the larger, more permanent settlements and more secure food supply, a somewhat more elaborate social system involving bandwide fraternities was present.

Most groups in the region, in response to the drier conditions and more meager food supply, were strikingly nomadic, and in the poorest niches the subsistence group was reduced to individual families for extended periods. Territoriality tended to be prominent in areas of abundant foods, weak where food resources were poor. In the Great Basin and the Southwest, piñon nuts and cacti were key resources; in the Plateau, roots and salmon. All groups used a variety of ground and chipped stone tools, and one of the distinctive artifacts was the milling stone for grinding seeds. Particularly characteristic was food storage, in basketry containers.

4. Chilean Shellfish Collectors

This is a generally poor environment, and even the primary food—shellfish—tended to fluctuate considerably in quantity. Bands in the area were small, completely migratory, and characterized by weakly developed territoriality and fluid membership.

5. Pampean—Patagonian Hunters

Guanaco and rhea are the most abundant animal foods in this area. Bands were completely migratory, generally of large size (40–120 people), with well-defined territoriality. Hunting tended to be communal and based on two tools, the bow and bolas. Chipped stone was the basic tool material, and the technology included an extensive use of skin for clothing, containers, and portable lean-to shelters.

6. Tropical Forest—Savanna Hunters and Gatherers

The vast Eastern Lowlands of South America were occupied, in 1492, by groups that may be classified as tropical farmers and will be more fully treated at a later point. A few, particularly in the Gran Chaco, were hunters and gatherers. The remainder were apparently hunters and gatherers who engaged in incipient cultivation only a few centuries before the conquest. The tropical farmers spoke primarily languages of the Equatorial phylum, the incipient cultivators and the hunters and gatherers were primarily Macro-Ge or Macro-Carib speakers. We noted the generally poor food resources for hunters and gatherers, the Chaco excepted. Basically, the pattern seems to have been one of prolonged seasonal occupation of riverine campsites by relatively large bands followed by seasons of dispersal (during rainy seasons) into the grasslands in small bands. When hunting and gathering groups became incipient cultivators, they changed their life way only slightly, simply adding agriculture to activities of the river camp. In contrast to tropical farmers, described below, the incipient cultivators lacked dugout canoes and did not use the rivers extensively as transportation systems. Some groups along the coast and major rivers also gathered shellfish. The subsistence pattern was basically a generalized one, including heavy reliance on both plants and animals.

Cultural Diversity: Tribes

New World *tribes* were found in four major culture areas, the Eastern Woodlands, the Southwest, the Tropical Lowlands of South America, and the Southern Andes. All groups in these areas shared the social and economic features noted in our analysis of this type; all were farmers, used pottery, and made tools of chipped and ground stone, bone, and wood; all lacked metallurgy, with the exception of those in the Southern Andes, who used copper and bronze tools; and all lived in substantial houses grouped in neighborhoods or villages. In three areas—the Southwest, the Tropical Forest, and the Southern Andes—loom-woven cloth was made. Craftsmanship was competent but not artistically unusual. With respect to religion, shamanism and the rites of life crisis continued to be important, but were combined with agricultural rites, rites of theoretical descent groups, and war rituals, frequently with pantribal participation. Warfare was much more important and generally tended to be of the commando, ambush, and raid type, frequently accompanied by cannibalism or trophy-taking. This was particularly true of the Eastern Woodlands and Tropical Forest areas.

More specific features of the four areas are summarized as follows:

1. Tropical Forest Farmers

There was a strikingly riparian orientation to this culture. The subsistence pattern included swidden [6] cultivation along flood plains of major rivers, with manioc as a staple, combined with river or coastal fishing, gathering, and hunting. Over most of the region bitter manioc was processed into flour and consumed as griddle cakes; in some areas sweet manioc was eaten as a cooked root. Dugout canoes were used in the rivers and the latter were main arteries of travel for visiting, warfare, trade, and migration. Settlements were of pole and thatch houses, and either were strung in linear bands along rivers or consisted of compact, often stockaded, villages in riverine or coastal locations. There was a strong tendency to reside in large, communal lineage houses. Social structure throughout the region tended to be of the loose, amorphous type, and tribes were commonly little more than nonaggression pacts.

---

[6] For a discussion of swidden systems, see pp. 41–42.

2. Southern Andes

This is a large complex region that includes high plateaus, mountain valleys, coastal deserts, Mediterranean valleys, and, in south central Chile, a small area of mixed latitude forest. Atacameno and Diaguita resided in the drier north, Araucanians in the more humid south. Subsistence was based on a combination of maize and potato cultivation and the herding of llamas and alpacas. Agriculture was intensive, involving irrigation and terracing in the north, and swidden in type in the far south. Water resources were thinly distributed and limited in the north. Villages, built of stone houses, tended to be compact, varying in size from lineage communities to large multi-lineage villages, according to the abundance of water. In any case, villages were widely spaced, and the total population was small. In the south, houses were of pole and thatch, and were dispersed; the density of population was heavier. In the north, communities were socially and politically autonomous; in the south, clusters of lineage neighborhoods were organized into loose tribes.

3. Southwestern Farmers

Sandwiched in among hunters and gatherers and incipient culti-vators in the southwestern part of the United States were a number of agricultural groups. These resided in three geographical niches: the Gila River Basin, the Colorado Valley and Plateau; and the Rio Grande Valley and Plateau. All combined maize cultivation with hunting and gathering of the desert type (in the last-named area, agriculture was of greater im-portance); all planted cotton and used woven cotton cloth. The Gila River Basin was occupied by the Pima, desert irrigators. They resided in small compact villages of separate earth and wood houses under village headmen and had an unusually centralized tribal government with its own hereditary headman. One major function of village and tribal headmen was the or-ganization of labor for canal construction and maintenance.

The Colorado Yumans lived in a similar niche, but planted crops in the humid soil of the floodplain following the annual flood. Their settlement pattern and political structure were similar to those of the Pima. The Anasazi (or Pueblos) resided in the plateau region of northern Arizona and the adjacent Rio Grande Valley in New Mexico. They resided in large, terraced, multilineage villages of conjoined stone and adobe rooms, an entire tribe housed in a single village. Rainfall is higher in the plateau, and some Anasazi agriculture was based entirely on it. More commonly, they cultivated alluvial fans at the base of canyon walls or used small, spring-based irrigation systems. Although the Anasazi possessed sibs, village inte-gration of an extraordinary intensity was achieved primarily by a complex system of religious fraternities. Religion was a major area of elaboration in Anasazi culture, and centered primarily on worship of ancestral beings with rainmaking and fecundity functions. Throughout the region, the amount of both water and suitable land for cultivation was limited, and the population density was low.

Geographically this is three regions. With respect to human adaptation, a distinction should be made between the forested eastern two-thirds of the area and the western third with its grass cover, and between the northeastern forests with their very severe winters and the southeast with its generally balmy winters. Some archaeologists have split the region into three culture areas, but the history of the three is so tightly interrrelated that for historical purposes it is better to consider the region a single unit.

All groups combined agriculture with hunting and gathering. Generally, agriculture was swidden in type, based on maize, and was most significant in the milder, forested Southeast. Although there was a certain preference for cultivation of the river floodplains, the strikingly linear distribution of population of the Tropical Farmers was only slightly approximated in this region. In the grassy plains cultivation was limited to the gallery forests. Villages broke up seasonally (in summer, following planting) in bands to hunt buffalo. The Plains groups can almost be said to have had two co-existent technologies and subsistence patterns. During the hunt they shifted from substantial log and earth houses to portable skin tepees, and from pottery to skin containers. Although much of the Eastern Woodlands is cultivable, population density in 1492 was surprisingly low, lower even than in the arid Southwest. House types varied in size from nuclear family to lineage residences, and in construction from bark and pole in the Northeast to grass, wattle, and daub in the Southeast. Settlements varied considerably in nucleation and size. Many Eastern Woodland tribes were highly organized multicommunity societies integrated by theoretical descent groups, associations, tribal religious ceremonies, and councils of tribal headmen.

Cultural Diversity: Chiefdoms and States

Chiefdoms occurred primarily in a huge continuous area that runs from Nicaragua to Ecuador. The region fits into James's complex mountain type; chiefdoms in the area represented an extraordinary variety of ecological adaptations. The region lies between the two great civilizations of Mesoamerica and the Central Andes; variable patterns of historical contacts between it and those regions add another complicating dimension. The culture area is known as the Intermediate area, in reference to its intermediate geographical and evolutionary position with respect to the two civilizations. The features we have described as characteristic of chiefdoms generally apply to the region; most of the distinctive features are social and religious. Special technological characteristics include metallurgy in gold, silver, and copper, although chipped and ground stone tools were used for most of the utilitarian artifacts; cotton and wool weaving; and ceramics, used for a variety of artifacts aside from pottery, such as figurines and stamps. The general level of craftsmanship was considerably higher than that found in tribes. In most areas, monumental architecture of earth and stone—primarily in the form of elite houses, tombs, and temples—was characteristic.

Maize was the staple crop over most of the area, shifting to potatoes in higher elevations and combined with manioc on the coastal plains. Systems of farming varied considerably, but agriculture was everywhere the main subsistence source. In the humid lowlands, various kinds of swidden were practiced; in the highlands, terracing and contour hoeing; and in more arid segments of the region, small-scale irrigation was typical.

Chiefdoms were also found in a number of other regions: the Caribbean culture area (West Indies and Venezuela north of the Orinoco); northwestern Mexico along the margin of the high civilization of Mesoamerica; the Lower Mississippi Valley, Gulf Coast, and South Atlantic coastal plains, within the Eastern Woodland area; and scattered localities within the Tropical Forest culture area.

All the above chiefdoms were based on agriculture. On the Pacific coast of Canada the native culture offers a notable exception to the association of hunting and gathering subsistence with band societal type. The natives harvested and stored enormous quantities of fish in a manner analogous to agricultural harvests. They were organized in tiny chiefdoms, each composed of a single lineage that resided in a large communal plank house. The lineage chief owned houses and fishing sites. A number of chiefs and their associated lineages resided in a single village. Since lineage chiefs within a village were ranked, each village could be considered a chiefdom. But even the largest village-chiefdoms included only a few hundred members.

Northwest Coast technology included an extraordinary elaboration of woodworking: huge dugout canoes, carved heraldic crests, boxes, and eating utensils. The basic tool kit heavily emphasized ground and polished stone.

States were found in only two culture areas. One area, Mesoamerica, included central and southern Mexico, Guatemala, Salvador, western Honduras, and British Honduras. The other, the Central Andes, included the highlands of Bolivia and highlands and coast of Peru.

Environmentally, both these culture areas are typical of James's complex mountain type and show both striking similarities and differences. In the Central Andes there are three major ecological niches, and each was utilized in a distinctive manner. Above 3600 meters are extensive rolling punas or grasslands, too high for growing most New World crops. They were used for llama and alpaca breeding and for cultivation of a variety of root and grain crops adapted to this elevation, particularly potatoes and quinoa. The Pacific coastal plain was a desert interrupted at intervals by fertile oases, intensively cultivated by means of large-scale irrigation from exotic rivers. Most of the culture area is composed of a complex series of mountain valleys and basins that lie between 1500 and 3400 meters above sea level, with highly variable climates and topography. Agriculture within this region was intensive and based on a combination of small-scale irrigation, dry farming, terracing, and slope-contouring.

In Mesoamerica the first two components of the Central Andean ecosystem had little significance. The third is directly comparable to the Mesoamerican Highlands in both its geographical characteristics and human adaptation. There are, however, differences. Mesoamerican valleys have larger plains and less rugged walls, and are generally drier than their Central Andean counterparts. In Mesoamerica we find one environmental type that was lacking in the Central Andes: the tropical forested lowlands, with an associated ecological system, based on swidden cultivation and orchard crops.

With the exception of those crops adapted to the highest Central Andean niche, there was considerable overlap in crop complexes in the two areas. Maize was the staple in Mesoamerica and on the Peruvian coast, and a co-staple in the intermediate mountain zone of the Central Andes. Both culture areas shared the basic characteristics we have defined for states. But they also differed strikingly in specific features of their respective technologies, economies, sociopolitical systems, and religion. In the following chapters these differences will be discussed in some detail.

In looking at the distribution of Service's societal types as a whole, one is struck by the obvious geographic symmetry. The two most complex levels —chiefdoms and states—are found primarily in a continuous zone from northwestern Mexico to the Bolivian–Argentine border. Archaeologists have referred to this huge region as Nuclear America. Tribal societies ring this area on the north, east, and south, whereas bands are found primarily in peripheral locations at both ends of the double continent. These distributions obviously point to critical problems in New World culture history.

Basic Problems
of New World History

There emerge four major problem areas of New World archaeology:

1. The first is that of the origin of the New World population in a biological sense. There can be no question, on paleontological and primatological evidence, that man originated in the Old World. The major questions then are: when, why, how, and from where did he migrate.

2. We noted the ubiquitous association of the band social type with a hunting and gathering subsistence and the association of agriculture with tribes, chiefdoms, and states. It is obvious, then, that the food-producing revolution paved the way for evolution of more complex societies in the New World. The origin, diffusion, and history of agriculture therefore remains one of the critical problems of New World archaeology.

3. Just as surely, the history of agriculture alone provides but a partial answer to such questions as why and how the more elaborate societal levels— chiefdoms and, particularly, states—evolved. Why were states found only in Mesoamerica and the Central Andes? Why not in the Intermediate area? Why were chiefdoms the common societal type in this last area?

4. The fourth problem area is that of defining the factors and processes of evolution of the culture of each culture area.

The solution of these problems will be of enormous help in the search for generalizations about cultural variation and dynamics, which is usually the fundamental preoccupation of archaeology.

In the pages to follow an outline of New World history will be presented. Chapter Three will deal with colonization of the New World by hunting and gathering bands, and then trace the history of adaptation of these groups to the varied New World environments. In Chapter Four the origins of New World agriculture will be discussed. In the subsequent three chapters, effects of the Food-Producing Revolution will be explored within various New World areas; in the final chapter, we will return to the theoretical contributions of New World archaeology.

Three Hunting
and Gathering Bands

Accepting the hypothesis that man evolved in the Old World and migrated to the Americas, the most obvious specific point of departure is Siberia.[1] The Bering Straits are less than 100 km wide and are today easily crossed by Eskimo using skin boats. During phases of glacial advance much water was locked up as ice, sea levels dropped, and a land bridge connected Siberia and Alaska, facilitating the crossing even further. During much of the Wisconsin glaciation, an ice-free corridor was available from northeastern Siberia, up the Yukon Valley, and along the eastern edge of the Canadian Rockies. Elsewhere, the enormous expanse of the Atlantic and Pacific must have acted as a significant barrier, at least in the early phases of population movement.

[1] For a more detailed picture of the contents of this chapter the reader may wish to consult Jesse D. Jennings and Edward Norbeck, eds., *Prehistoric Man in the New World* (Chicago: The University of Chicago Press, 1963); Edward P. Lanning, "Early Man in Peru," *Scientific American*, CCXIII, 4 (1965), pp. 68–76; Betty J. Meggers and Clifford Evans, eds., *Aboriginal Culture Development in Latin America: An Interpretive Review*, Smithsonian Miscellaneous Collections, vol. 146, no. 1 (Washington: Smithsonian Institution, 1963); H. M. Wormington, *Ancient Man in North America*, 4th ed., Popular Series No. 4 (Denver: Denver Museum of Natural History, 1957); and Gordon R. Willey, *An Introduction to American Archaeology*, vol. 1: North and Middle America (Englewood Cliffs, N.J.: Prentice-Hall, Inc., 1966).

Physically, American Indians are generally classified as Mongoloids. This race evolved in northeastern Asia in adaptation to conditions of extreme cold. The most Mongoloid-looking Indians are found in the extreme Northwest among Eskimo and Na-Dene speakers. However, all groups have a veneer of Mongoloid traits. Skeletal evidence from archaeological sites indicates that the earliest immigrants lacked the cold-adapted specializations so characteristic of historic Siberian natives. The more specialized Mongoloids arrived later. Presumably, the veneer of Mongoloid traits found in southern groups is a product of later gene flow from north to south. Many of the minor physical variations found among American Indian groups were the product of subsequent adaptation to various environmental niches of the New World.

Linguistic evidence also seems to point to two basic waves of population movement. The earliest wave apparently occurred as a series of closely spaced phases of colonization that brought, in succession, the Macro-Carib-Ge, the Macro-Arawakan and Macro-Quechuan (the Andean–Equatorial group), and the Macro-Maya superphyla. None of these languages has any acknowledged relationship to Asiatic languages, which suggests a movement of considerable antiquity. The second wave occurred much later and brought first the Na-Dene, then the Eskimo. Vague relationships have been suggested between this wave and the Ural–Altaic or Sinitic.

In summary, both physical and linguistic evidence points to two population movements from Siberia, both of considerable time depth. The earlier occurred prior to evolution of the specialized Mongoloid type in Siberia and produced the bulk of New World population. The later migration must have occurred relatively early as well, certainly prior to the evolution of productive agriculture; otherwise, the demographic disparity engendered by agriculture would certainly have acted as a barrier to the spread of Mongoloid genes southward.

Pioneer Hunters and Gatherers

The earliest definite evidence of man in the New World dates from about 10,000 B.C. Tool complexes from this period represent a culture already well adapted to the New World environment. Furthermore, the specific artifact styles have no counterpart in Asia, which suggests a much earlier colonization of the New World—either during one of the Interstadials of the Wisconsin Glaciation or during the preceding Sangamon Interglacial. A number of archaeologists have claimed discovery of remains of these earlier immigrants, but all these claims are in dispute. The industries in question involve crude, percussion-flaked tools, scrapers, flakes, and pebble-choppers; Krieger [2] assigns them to what he calls the Pre-Projectile Point stage or horizon, owing to the absence of the projectile point so characteristic of the earliest well-documented archaeological complexes. Disagreement centers primarily on the identification of the objects as artifacts or on their supposed association with either geologically ancient strata or extinct Pleistocene animals.

---

[2] Alex D. Krieger, "The Pre-Projectile Point Stage," in Jennings and Norbeck, *op. cit.*, pp. 23–84.

Charcoal samples from supposed hearths in North American sites have been found (by C14 method) to date from between 38,000 and 22,000 years ago. None of these claims has been fully accepted by American archaeologists. The most convincing case is from Lake Maracaibo in South America. A small river—the Pedernales—flows into the lake. During the Wisconsin Glaciation in North America the stream gradually eroded its bed, leaving a series of four terraces, each associated with stone industries. The oldest is referred to as Camare and is associated with the uppermost terrace. The industry is exceedingly crude and includes percussion-flaked choppers and scrapers; there are no projectile points. West of Lake Maracaibo a similar complex, called Manzanillo, has been reported. No C14 dates have been reported for either, but dates varying from 14,500 to 12,000 B.C. have been associated with the El Jobo industry, which is later, dating from the cutting of the third terrace.

The tools in question fairly closely resemble those from sites in Siberia that range from the Sangamon Interglacial to earlier phases of the Wisconsin Glaciation. The earliest migration indicated by biological and linguistic evidence presumably occurred during this period. Although most writers have favored an entry during phases of glacial advance when the land bridge was available, we would favor migration during the warmer Interglacial or Interstadials since the artifact complex indicates a relatively unspecialized hunting and gathering subsistence that lacked Arctic and sub-Arctic specializations. The migrants probably first colonized the immediate northwestern North American region. Hunters and Gatherers do not normally migrate over great distances, and the subsequent history can be pictured as one of almost imperceptible movement southward stimulated by gradual changes in flora and fauna—and hence food supply—produced by the stadial advances. In summary, the earliest migrants were generalized hunters and gatherers, with a band level of social organization. As they spread south, their culture gradually changed in response to the varied New World environment. We will now briefly summarize the history of these adaptations.

Hunters of the Great Plains

The rolling grassy plains of the center of the United States were a game paradise during the pre-European period. By approximately 10,000 B.C., a number of bands had developed a subsistence system based on hunting of megafauna of the region, particularly bison and mammoth. A number of stylistic phases of this adaptation, based on projectile points, have been defined: Clovis (10,000–9000 B.C.), Folsom (9000–7000 B.C.), and Plano (7000–5000 B.C.). The dates are based on a mass of convincing evidence: association with datable geological strata, with extinct Pleistocene fauna, and with radiocarbon-dated samples. In contrast to the tools from the Pre-Projectile Point stage, the artifacts are technically excellent; their identification as tools is unimpeachable. Most finds are from sites where animals were killed and butchered; very few campsites have been located and excavated.

The tools consist of lanceolate-shaped spear points, leaf-shaped knives, and small scrapers for fleshing hides—all well made of chipped stone; crudely flaked multi-purpose choppers; and awls, needles, spatulas, and fleshing tools

—all fashioned of bone. The parallel in technology to summer hunting bands of the historic Plains Indians is a very close one, and one can draw on the ethnography of these groups to complete an account of the Early Hunters. Like most of their historic counterparts, the latter were probably organized into relatively large, patrilocal, territorial bands that hunted big game for food, clothing, containers, and shelter. They undoubtedly used the historic technique of communal hunting in which herds were surrounded and panicked into topographic cul-de-sacs or driven over bluffs, and dispatched with stabbing spears. Some writers have argued that the subsistence base was actually a more generalized one and that the big-game sector of the subsistence has been grossly overemphasized. In fact, evidence of numerous kill sites, the extinction of a great number of Pleistocene animals by 7000 B.C., and the fact that the type of environment of most of the region during the early phases of the tradition (tundra grassland and boreal forest) is poor in resources other than game, all indicate a big-game focus.

Clovis and Folsom points are characterized by a peculiar fluting on each face. Clovis points are larger and more crudely made. They are also more widely distributed, being found in the Great Plains, western margins of the plains, and over most of the eastern United States. Folsom points are limited to the western part of the region; in the east, the cruder Clovis type continued. The term Plano refers to a great variety of unfluted leaf-shaped points that are everywhere later than fluted points. In some varieties the flaking is superbly done. They are found in the Plains, the Plains margins, and in the Great Lakes region.

From 5000 to 3000 B.C. a climatic phase referred to as the Altithermal became established over much of the United States and Mexico. It was characterized by warmer and drier conditions than prevail at present. The Southwest and Great Basin were converted to deserts, and the great herds of bison dwindled in the plains to a level that made a big-game hunting economy impossible. The subsequent return to the moister and colder conditions that are found today stimulated the development of a great variety of new types of band adaptation.

Forest Hunters and Gatherers

Fluted points of a general Clovis type have been found in most eastern states; in all probability, groups utilizing them in the southeast had a hunting and gathering economy, less specialized than that of the Big-Game Hunters of the Plains. During the Valders Stadial this region had a forest cover comparable to that of the contemporary northeastern United States, and this environmental type has abundant plant foods. As the Valders ice sheet retreated, present-day climatic conditions gradually appeared over the region. Beginnings of an adaptation to a mid-latitude mixed forest, then, were probably initiated in the southeast during the Valders advance and gradually spread north in post-Pleistocene times. Specialists in Eastern Woodland archaeology refer to this new adaptation as the Archaic.

The new way of life was based on a combination of hunting, fishing, and shellfish collection along the coast and major rivers, and on wild-plant collecting, particularly of such nuts as acorn and hickory. Nuts were harvested and stored in much the same manner as that in which historic Californians used to store acorns and grass seeds. The variety of wild plants available and used by historic Great Lake Indians in this niche is impressive. Griffin cites a list of 130 plants used for food alone, from a total list of 558.[3]

This thorough utilization of the environment has been referred to by Caldwell as Primary Forest Efficiency. Caldwell lists as major technological innovations that permitted such a level of adaptation: throwing spears with chipped stone points characterized by notched or stemmed bases; spear-throwers, to increase velocity and range of the spear; spear-thrower weights of polished stone, to obtain greater stability and depth of penetration; ground and pecked milling stones, to process seeds and nuts; heavy woodworking tools like ground stone axes, celts, adzes, and gouges; bone tools for fishing; and stone vessels for cooking.[4] He argues that the shift from fluted points to notched points reflects a change from communal hunting of large herds of migratory game to individual stalking and tracking of nonmigratory forest animals that grouped in small numbers. The basic technique of forest hunting consists of striking game from close range with the throwing-spear and subsequent tracking of the wounded animal. The notched base point insures that the spear remains embedded in the animal, thus slowing him down.

Archaic sites vary from temporary camps to relatively sedentary settlements, the latter primarily along major rivers where a combination of shellfish gathering, hunting, and wild-seed and nut gathering permitted protracted residence. In all probability, macrobands gathered seasonally at such sites, then dispersed into microbands during much of the year.

The Archaic tradition has been segmented historically into three phases, Early (7000–5000 B.C.), Middle (5000–2000 B.C.) and Late (2000–1000 B.C.). During the Early phase the only item present in Caldwell's inventory was the notched projectile point. The Middle Archaic phase witnessed the appearance of a great variety of ground stone tools. The Late Archaic is defined according to Willey by appearance of pottery in Carolina–Georgia piedmont sites.[5] The pottery is fiber-tempered, crudely made, and soft; it is the first pottery in North America north of Mexico, and appears to be a local invention, since forms imitate those of Middle Archaic stone bowls.

Montane Hunters and Gatherers

The characteristic fluted and plano points have been reported in a few scattered localities in the Southwest and west of the Rockies. Geographically, this region contrasts sharply with the Great Plains and the Eastern Woodlands. Essentially it is a subhumid-to-arid region of narrow coastal plains, mountains, valleys, and plateaus. The most abundant wild foods are plant foods. These vary strikingly in density, and variety depends on variability of relief and degree of aridity. During the Wisconsin Glaciation, the drier sections were relatively lush. A gradual dessication of the region, reach-

[3] James B. Griffin, "Eastern North American Archaeology: A Summary," *Science*, vol. 156 (1967), pp. 175–192.
[4] Joseph R. Caldwell, *Trend and Tradition in the Prehistory of the Eastern United States*, Memoir 88 (Menasha, Wisc.: American Anthropological Association, 1958).
[5] Willey, *op. cit.*, pp. 257–258.

ing its nadir around 5000 B.C., followed the Valders advance. Since then there have been modifications towards the slightly more moist conditions of today.

From 9000 to 7000 B.C. conditions were still relatively favorable for a human population, even in drier sections. Widespread over the region at this time was a culture, or series of related cultures, referred to as Old Cordilleran. Most excavated sites are caves located in the plateau region of Oregon and Washington, southern California, Utah, and Nevada. The Central Plateau and adjacent mountains of Mexico are comparable in environmental characteristics, and related cultures have been defined in the Basin of Mexico, the Sierra de Tamaulipas, and the Tehuacan Valley.

The distinctive artifact is a bipointed leaf-shaped spear point. Other artifacts include choppers, large scrapers, and crude, unmodified flake tools. In Gypsum Cave, Nevada, the complex is associated with bones of extinct camels and ground sloths; in Tamaulipas and Tehuacan, with bones of modern varieties of deer and antelope along with an extinct horse. The Basin of Mexico variant is associated with mammoths. Still, the complex is much more commonly associated with hunting of small animals. The subsistence pattern has been described as a generalized hunting and gathering one. It lacked both the extreme specialization for big game characteristic of Clovis and Folsom and the extreme dependence on collection of wild plants characteristic of northern portions of the region in historic times. After 7000 B.C. the present variable geographical conditions were established, temporarily interrupted by the dry altithermal. These changes appear to have stimulated rapid diversification of distinctive lifeways that produced the historic cultural variation found in the region. The various local cultures can be grouped into three broad subregional traditions: Desert, Plateau, and Californian.

The Desert Tradition evolved in southern California, the Great Basin, and the southwestern United States. The major solution to problems posed by survival in the desert was development of a subsistence pattern based on wild plants. The various types of plants in this region are found in different microgeographical niches (valley floor, lower slopes, middle slopes) and vary in production by season, thus necessitating periodic shifts in residence. They are also thinly distributed and erratic in yield, conditions that put severe limits on band size, encourage relatively fluid band membership, and place a premium on food storage. Hunting was primarily restricted to small animals in historic times, slow game (lizards, tortoises), and rabbits. The latter were driven into long, fence-like nets and either clubbed to death with throwing-clubs or lanced with throwing spears.

Basic tools for these activities were the throwing-spear with a notched base, chipped stone point; spear-throwers; throwing-clubs; milling stones for grinding seeds and nuts; choppers and scrapers for pulping fibers and fleshing skins; digging sticks for prying up roots; cordage for nets and bags; and a great variety of baskets for storing food and water, winnowing grain, and preparing food. All these have been found by archaeologists in the dry caves of the region, in some areas dated as early as 8000 B.C. The pattern became well established over most of the region by 7000 B.C.

Between 3000 and 2000 B.C., a primitive type of maize appears, and the subsistence pattern includes incipient cultivation. However, this additional source of food played a minor role in the life way of Desert peoples until around the time of Christ. Desert-adapted hunters and gatherers or incipient cultivators continued to live in some portions of the region up to historic times. Subsequent changes were primarily of a stylistic nature, with the exception of a gradual replacement of the spear by the bow. The extreme characteristics of the region required a rapid initial adaptation and subsequent stabilization. The archaeology indicates that this did happen.

The plateau between the Rockies and the coastal ranges in Washington and Oregon has a climatic regime less extreme than the Desert Province and is better characterized as a steppe or elevated semiarid grassland. Plant and animal food resources are more abundant; and an additional resource is found in salmon from the Colombia and Snake river systems. Changing conditions of the post-Pleistocene did not require the drastic reorientation of subsistence discernible in the Desert Province; instead, the culture between 5000 B.C. and historic times was essentially a continuation of the Old Cordilleran lifeway. The Altithermal did, however, act as a stimulus toward an increasing reliance on river fishing as opposed to land hunting, which was combined with the collection of plant foods, particularly seeds and roots. The richness of river resources also stimulated a sort of seasonal sedentarianism comparable to that of the Archaic Hunters and Gatherers of the east.

A succession of local chronological sequences has been worked out for the region; these may be subsumed under three periods: Period I (8000–4100 B.C.) is essentially the Old Cordilleran tradition. The shift towards salmon fishing was already underway toward the end of this period. Period II (4100–1500 B.C.) witnessed replacement of leaf-shaped points by notched and stemmed points and the appearance of ground stone milling stones. Period III (1500 B.C.–historic) began with the introduction of a variety of ground stone tools: mauls, tubular pipes, spear-thrower weights, gorgets, fishnet weights, mortars and pestles, fish gorges, and zoomorphic sculptures—all characteristic of historic Salishan cultures of the region.

The narrow coastal plains, mountain slopes, and valleys of California offer ideal conditions for a hunting and gathering population. The history of adaptation to this environment is essentially one of increasing population and more thorough utilization of the varied resources, leading ultimately to evolution of a variety of microecological systems. These may be grouped into two types: *maritime,* based on sea mammals and shell fish, and *inland,* based primarily on gathering of acorns and wild seeds (but including river fishing and land hunting as well). The basic tool kit included baskets; milling stones; spears with chipped stone, stemmed, and notched-base points; spear-throwers; barbed-bone fish spears; shell hooks; and plank boats.

Unusually heavy population (two to five per sq. km in some areas), sedentary village settlements, food surpluses, and a tendency for natural resources to be found in selected niches all stimulated part-time specialization and extensive trade, to an extent normally associated with tribal societies. Characteristic of the archaeological assemblages is a great elaboration of non-utilitarian artifacts of stone, bone, and shell—primarily for bodily ornaments. The combination of complex topography and highly parochial social structure with hundreds of autonomous sedentary bands led to considerable stylistic variation from area to area.

Heizer has combined these local sequences into an overall chronological scheme for Californian history. It, too, consists of three periods: Early (5000–2000 B.C.), Middle (2000 B.C.–A.D. 250), and Late (A.D. 250–Historic).[6] During the Early Period the specific historical local adaptations were lacking, and population was small. The historic Californian pattern seems to have been well established by the Middle Period. Technological innovations in the Late Period include pottery (diffused from the Southwest) and the bow.

Arctic and Subarctic Hunters

We noted the biological and linguistic evidence that suggests a late arrival in the New World of the Na-Dene and Eskimo languages. In historic times, the former were found primarily in western interior Canada, the latter on the Arctic coast. The evidence would also suggest that each group was the product of separate population movements. Whether the specialized Eskimo adaptation to the coast evolved in situ in North America or whether the Siberian immigrants had already evolved this ecosystem in Asia, prior to migration, is a major debate in Arctic archaeology.

With the exception of a few scattered finds of tools similar to those of the Old Cordilleran tradition, the first evidence of occupation of the Arctic–Subarctic region is a chipped stone industry called the Northwest Microblade tradition. It includes small blades struck from conical and tongue-shaped cores, as well as burins, knives, scrapers, and a variety of spear points. Sites are located primarily inland. Subsistence was based on land animal hunting, particularly buffalo, elk, and caribou. Dates range from 6500 to 3500 B.C. in Alaska and from 5500 to 1000 B.C. in the Yukon territory. The historic Na-Dene Forest culture probably evolved directly out of it. Later additions included a variety of ground stone woodworking tools and the bow. The earlier dates from Alaska, as well as the similarity of the industry to blade industries of the Siberian Mesolithic, strongly suggest that a migration from Siberia brought the Northwest Microblade tradition into North America.

The first truly Arctic Coastal tradition appeared on the Alaskan shore between 4000 and 3000 B.C. and is referred to as the Arctic Small Tool tradition. It resembled historic Eskimo culture in the emphasis on coastal residence and in its caribou-walrus hunting pattern. Lacking, however, were such evolved Eskimo adaptations as substantial winter houses, oil lamps, and emphasis on ground slate and ivory tools. Skin boats were undoubtedly used, but sleds probably were not. The tool kit was composed of chipped stone produced by a blade technique from polyhedral cores and included arrow points (used to hunt caribou), small retouched crescent-shaped blades that were inserted in bone heads and used as spears (to hunt walrus), burins, and knives.

This coastal lifeway diffused eastward into the eastern Arctic after 1000 B.C., where it is known as Dorset. Dorset sites in the east, dating from between 800 and 600 B.C., offer evidence of skin tents, oil lamps, combinations of chipped stone, ground slate and bone in a variety of tools (some of which

---

[6] Robert F. Heizer, "The Western Coast of North America," in Jennings and Norbeck, *op. cit.*, pp. 117–148.

stylistically resemble the older industry), bone harpoons with slotted stone barbs for hunting seals, and sleds.

A fully Eskimo lifeway began in Saint Lawrence Island by 300 B.C. The technological inventory includes the winter house; ivory, bone, and ground stone tools; composite harpoons; pottery oil lamps; skin boats; tailored garments; and hand-drawn sleds. A variety of chipped stone tools were still in use in the earliest phase (Okvik). By Punuk times (1000 A.D.) chipped stone tools had virtually disappeared, and dog-drawn sleds were added, along with special whaling harpoons, iron-tipped tools (the iron imported by trade from Siberia), and sinew-backed bows. This more highly evolved Arctic coastal culture diffused eastward, probably by small-scale migration (we noted the absence of territoriality and fluid band membership of the historic Eskimo), replacing the older Dorset culture.

In summary, evidence from Arctic archaeology indicates that a new migration from Siberia, around 4000 B.C. brought to Alaska ancestors of the Eskimo who were bearers of a specialized Arctic coastal subsistence pattern. By 300 B.C., this new pattern continued to evolve—probably with later periodic influences from Asia (the product of subsequent small-scale migrations)—into the specialized Eskimo culture.

Montane Hunters
and Gatherers of the South

Assuming that most of the New World population was derived from Siberia, the South American continent should logically have been occupied later. The South American counterparts of the Montane tradition of the western United States are at least of comparable antiquity, indicating that colonization took place prior to the Valders ice advance in the north. We noted evidence of a Pre-Projectile Point stage in the Lake Maracaibo Basin and from surface finds farther south.

South America consists of four great regions: a complex mountain province along the western edge of the continent; a huge tropical lowland plain of savannas and tropical forests to the east; the rolling temperate grasslands of Argentina; and a maritime–boreal forest along the south Chilean coast. Each region would have posed different problems of cultural adaptation.

The Montane region, as defined here, includes the slopes, valleys, and plateaus of the Andes in addition to the adjacent Caribbean and Pacific coast plains. It is a region of great diversity and rich natural food resources, much of it comparable in this respect to California. In the highland niches, deer and wild ancestors of the llama and alpaca were abundant—in Pleistocene times, mammoths, mastodons, wild horses, and ground sloths—and the area offered excellent hunting possibilities. The wild ancestors of later highland grain and root crops provided plentiful plant food resources. Along the coast, shellfish, fish, and sea mammals were abundant. Rivers of the Caribbean and Ecuadorean coast offered an additional resource.

Archaeological evidence demonstrates that upland portions of the region were occupied by the close of the Pleistocene, and that the various groups had evolved a subsistence system comparable in many ways to the Old

Cordilleran culture and its derivatives in the North American Far West. Controlled archaeological data are available from four localities: Lake Maracaibo in Venezuela; Lauricocha, near Huancayo in the Peruvian Andes; the Ancón Valley on the Central Peruvian Coast; and Ayampitín and Ongamira Caves in northwestern Argentina. There is extraordinary stylistic similarity in certain tools from these widely spaced sites, accompanied by variation in other tools, the latter apparently related to specializations in subsistence patterns.

The Lauricocha sites consist of three stratified and excavated caves. The great elevation (4000 m above sea level) is understandable from a cultural– ecological point of view since the high punas (cold grasslands) were superior hunting areas, but it is surprising to find a hunting group biologically adapted to such a high elevation this early. Again it suggests a much earlier original colonization.

Cardich [7] has defined four phases of occupation. The last is ceramic and agricultural and will not concern us here. Lauricocha I (8000–6000 B.C.) includes crude, elongated, unifacially chipped points as well as steep-sided scrapers and crude, bifacially chipped, elongated and broad leaf-shaped points (probably spear points). Lauricocha II (6000–3000 B.C.) includes the same types but adds a finely retouched leaf-shaped point similar in many ways to Old Cordilleran points. It was first found in South America in Argentina and is referred to as the Ayampitín point. Also associated are large, bifacially flaked, stemmed points with triangular blades and bifacially flaked knives and knife-scrapers. In Lauricocha III (3000–1200 B.C.) there was a great reduction in projectile point size with small, well-chipped, bipointed points; small, finely chipped, leaf-shaped points; and a striking increase in bone tools. Mammal bones, particularly deer and wild llama, are found in all levels and become increasingly abundant. Milling stones are absent and the subsistence pattern apparently focused on hunting and possibly gathering of wild tubers. The reduction in point size might relate to a shift from use of stabbing-spears to that of throwing-spears.

The Central Coast of Peru topographically consists of a series of small transverse valleys each bordered by low ranges of hills or lomas. Today many of these valleys are dry, including the Ancón Valley. During the Wisconsin Glaciation rainfall was heavier in the neighboring Andes, rivers had at least seasonal water, and the lomas were covered with a type of succulent desert vegetation. This was supported by dense fogs of the type that invades the coast today—but apparently they brought more moisture then—during the highland dry season (April–November). During this period highland animals such as deer and wild llama migrated down to the lomas to feed on the fog-nurtured vegetation. Local fauna included owls, lizards, and land snails; plant foods included a variety of roots and seeds.

Highland-based hunters and gatherers apparently migrated down to the lomas seasonally, following game. Lanning has presented a detailed record of these movements from 7000–2500 B.C.[8] The tool kit included projectile

---

[7] Angus Cardich, "Lauricocha, Fundamentos para una Prehistoria de los Andes Centrales," *Studia Praehistoria*, III (Buenos Aires: Centro Argentino de Estudios Prehistoricos, 1964).

[8] Lanning, *op. cit.*, pp. 68–76.

points, comparable in style to those from Lauricocha; scrapers, knives, and awls for working skins; a variety of heavy chopping and pulping tools for processing plant fibers; and milling stones for grinding seeds. The subsistence pattern (at least during this season) was a combination of hunting and gathering.

For the semiarid mountain valleys and adjacent pampas of northwestern Argentina, Rex Gonzalez [9] has reported a hunting and gathering culture very similar to that from Ancón. It is called Ayampitín, dates from 6000–3000 B.C., and includes Ayampitín points, scrapers, knives, and ground stone milling stones. This is succeeded between 3000 and 500 B.C. by the Ongamira culture, similar in general features, but with a shift in projectile points to a great variety of smaller-stemmed and stemless points.

Lake Maracaibo cultures were more comparable to those from Lauricocha in the absence of milling stones and emphasis on hunting. Following the Camare phase was a succession of three phases, Las Lagunas, El Jobo, and Las Casitas. Las Lagunas and El Jobo are directly comparable in style and artifact inventory to Lauricocha I and II. Las Casitas is different stylistically, but comparable to Lauricocha III in projectile point-size reduction. If the C14 dates from El Muaco (not situated on the Rio Pedernales terraces) date the El Jobo point, the evolutive phases of the tradition are considerably earlier in Venezuela than in North America and are associated with Pleistocene fauna. More probably the dates pertain to Camare: the site of El Mauco is much disturbed and the association there of fauna, C14 samples, and artifacts not well established.[10]

In summary, following the retreat of the Valders Glacier in the north, we have evidence of a number of stylistically related cultures in the Montane region that differed in their specific environmental adaptation in response to the microgeographical complexity of the region. Differences in terminal dates of the tradition reflect variability of the appearance of agriculture in these highly distinctive ecological niches.

On the coastal plains of the Montane region and partly contemporary with highland hunters and gatherers were a series of cultures adapted to a littoral environment. Their remains are reported in the Greater Antilles, Venezuela, British Guiana, Colombia, Panama, Ecuador, Peru, and Chile. Individual groups varied in the style of their tools and in the presence or absence of such technological elaborations as pottery and twined cloth; but all show characteristics of prolonged seasonal residence in one locality (most sites consist of deep, extensive middens of earth and shell) and heavy reliance on shellfish. In some areas there was a marine orientation based on shellfish gathering and sea mammal hunting; in other areas sites were located near the mouths of rivers, and freshwater shellfish, reptiles, and mammals provided most of the food. All groups did some inland hunting and wild-plant collecting as well. Along the coast of Peru, even in the earliest phases of the history of the ecosystem, these subsistence activities were combined with incipient cultivation, but in other regions direct evidence of agriculture is absent, and archaeologists have defined a

[9] Alberto Rex Gonzalez, "Cultural Development in Northwestern Argentina," in Meggers and Evans, *op. cit.*, pp. 102–118.
[10] Irving Rouse, "The Caribbean Area," in Jennings and Norbeck, *op. cit.*, pp. 389–417.

long period of occupation of the coast prior to food production. We will therefore reserve discussion of the Peruvian sites for the chapters on agricultural origins and diffusion. Artifact inventories include a variety of crudely chipped stone tools, (but projectile points in many sites are absent); bone and shellfish-hooks and harpoons; and reamers and gravers for working the last two materials. In some sites ground-stone milling stones and woodworking tools are present.

In Ecuador, sites of the tradition, but including pottery, have been reported on the Pacific coast. Two separate ceramic stylistic traditions have been defined, Valdivia (divided into four phases) and Machalilla. Each is thought to result from separate migrations from outside. Meggers argues that Valdivia was the product of an accidental migration of a boatload of storm-driven fishermen from Japan.[11] Whatever its origin, the Valdivia tradition is dated by Meggers from 3200 to 1000 B.C., Machalilla from 2000 to 1500 B.C. Both traditions, following Meggers, were ultimately replaced from 1500 to 1000 B.C. by a new migration, that of farmers from Mesoamerica (Chorrera phase).

There is considerable room for skepticism concerning this reconstruction. The three ceramic traditions exhibit much more continuity than Meggers has allowed, suggesting a lineal relationship. On theoretical grounds alone her reconstruction of periodic migrations as the major process of culture change is a dubious one. Doubtless some changes in the coastal Ecuadorean sequence were due to external contacts, primarily trade. Nor do the C14 dates support her position. In Meggers's chart of C14 dates there are no Chorrera dates prior to 850 B.C., the only C14 date reported for Machalilla is 1370 B.C., and the latest Valdivia date (phase C) is 1500 B.C. Furthermore, the earliest C14 date for Valdivia (A) of 3200 B.C. is isolated from a cluster of Valdivia A dates that occur 500 years later. In short, the dates of the Coastal Ecuadorean sequence could be easily revised upward, with Valdivia extending from 2700 to 1400 B.C., Machalilla from 1400 to 900 B.C., and Chorerra from 900 to 500 B.C. These changes are of critical importance because her elongated chronology led Meggers to assume that Ecuador was unusually precocious in New World culture history and that much subsequent evolution of South American ceramics was the product of diffusion from that area. The chronology presented here would align the Ecuadorean sequence more closely with those of neighboring regions.

Ceramics appear at the beginning of the Littoral Tradition in Ecuador and are technically excellent, with a variety of vessel forms and decorative techniques, the latter almost entirely plastic. Hand-modeled clay figurines are characteristic of Valdivia B and C. Machalilla pottery is harder, with thinner walls, and includes a red-on-base bichrome as well as plastic decoration. Two new forms of considerable interest in terms of later events appear with Machalilla: the stirrup spout bottle and the composite silhouette bowl.

Reichel-Dolmatoff has defined a similar sequence on the Caribbean coast of Colombia, again accompanied by ceramics from its inception.[12] The subsistence may be characterized as river-mouth rather than marine. The

---

[11] Betty J. Meggers, *Ecuador* (New York: Frederick A. Praeger, Inc., 1966).
[12] Gerardo Reichel-Dolmatoff, *Colombia* (New York: Frederick A. Praeger, Inc., 1965).

ceramic tradition has been divided into two phases: the earliest, Puerto Hormiga, dates from 3000 to 1500 B.C.; the latest, Barlovento, 1500 to 1000 B.C. The sequence ends with the Malambo ceramic phase and the beginnings of agriculture. Puerto Hormiga pottery falls into two classes: very soft, crude undecorated, fiber-tempered ware; and harder, better fired, sand-tempered ware with plastic decoration. In specific forms and design it differs from Valdivia but resembles the latter in some decorative techniques. Barlovento is essentially a developmental phase out of Puerto Hormiga, retaining the emphasis on plastic decoration, but with a greater variety of design. Both Reichel-Dolmatoff and Meggers postulate the existence of preceramic littoral traditions in Colombia and Ecuador, but as yet there is no archaeological confirmation. Such a phase has been reported from Cerro Mongote in Panama with a C14 date of 4850 B.C. A nearby site in the same area, Monagrillo, continues the tradition but has pottery (appearing at least as early as 2130 B.C.).

In Venezuela ceramics and agriculture appear in local sequences together. Prior to this the coastal zone was occupied by at least two nonceramic littoral cultures: El Hineal and Manicuare. El Hineal, on the West Caribbean coast, may begin as early as 4000 B.C.; Manicuare, on the east coast, by 2500 B.C. The offshore islands were occupied from the beginning of the sequence, indicating use of boats; this is also suggested by the presence of heavy woodworking tools like shell gouges and celts. Some El Hineal and Manicuare fishermen, and possibly others from Panama, reached the larger West Indian islands by 1000 B.C. The littoral tradition on the Venezuela coast lasted in some areas as late as the time of Christ; in western Cuba it persisted until the Spanish Conquest. The littoral lifeway appeared as far south as the north Chilean coast by 3000 B.C. and continued there until the simultaneous appearance of agriculture and pottery around 500 B.C.

Tropical Lowland Hunters and Gatherers

Most cultural geographers have commented on the relatively poor wild food resources of the Tropical Forest environment. Savannas are usually much richer areas but South American savannas have an unusually poor fauna. The coast and rivers add an additional resource and we have noted their significance in the economy of both agricultural and nonagricultural historic groups. It is possible that the region was occupied later than the Montane, but the research done on this is spotty and only partially reported.

Some of the most controversial finds in American archaeology have been reported from limestone caves in Lagoa Santa, in the east Brazilian savannas. Lund in the 19th century reported bones of Pleistocene fauna and man along with human artifacts. In the 1930s and '40s Walters excavated a number of caves and defined four phases of occupation, two of which were preceramic; he also claimed definite association of the fauna with the human occupation. A C14 date from one early level recorded 1000 B.C. In 1956 Hurt excavated several caves, found no evidence of faunal association, and collapsed Walter's four phases into two, a preceramic Cerca Grande phase followed by a ceramic phase. He felt that both were late. Published C14 dates from Hurt's excavations, however, range from 7770 to 7076 B.C., thus reopening the question of possible extinct faunal associations.[13]

The tools differ strikingly from those in the Montane area. They include chipped stone arrowpoints; a variety of scrapers and choppers; pebble-grinding tools; celts, some completely ground, others flaked with ground edges; bone points and awls.

South of Lagoa Santa, in the savannas of São Paulo and Paraná, a series of similar stone and bone tools have been reported, ranging from 5000 B.C. to 1000 A.D. In both areas pottery and agriculture appear at the latter date.

Shell middens, some of huge size, are a characteristic feature of the east Brazilian coast from Paraná to the Amazon delta. Some represent detritus of occupation by the agricultural and pottery-making Tupi, who entered the area around 1000 A.D.; others are considerably older. Excavations in middens with preceramic occupations have produced C14 dates that range from 5900 B.C. (the oldest littoral-adapted culture in the New World) to 500 A.D. We have therefore a continuous record of a shellfish-gathering population for more than 6000 years; but none of the sites is fully reported. A partial list of artifacts from the Sambaquí Gomes (2500 B.C.) includes stone and bone projectile points and crude choppers, hammers, and scrapers. In the slightly later Sambaquí Saquarema (2300–2000 B.C.) percussion-flaked axes, some with polished bits, are reported in lower levels, completely ground celts in the upper.

The dates from the two areas are somewhat contradictory, and those from the coast cast doubt on the very early dates for ground celts at Cerca Grande. What *can* be said is that there is definite evidence of population in eastern South America by 6000 B.C., that two distinct eco-systems were well established by 4000 B.C., and that ceramics and agriculture appear very late in the sequence—after 1000 A.D. There may have been a riparian variant of the littoral ecosystem in interior areas at this time.

Grassland Hunters of Patagonia

The southern grasslands were occupied by a population of hunters at the time of the Spanish Conquest. Archaeological research, based on excavation in two caves in southern Argentina (Fells and Palli Aike) and surveys of many open air campsites, has demonstrated that this pattern of life appeared in the region as early as 9000 to 8000 B.C. and persisted with relatively minor changes until the historic period. At the two caves Bird[14] has defined five phases of occupation. Phase I includes a specialized form of chipped stone spearpoint with a concave base and two projecting ears (referred to as a fishtail point). They are associated with ground sloth and horse, the only case of definite association of Pleistocene fauna with man

---

[13] Wesley R. Hurt, "Recent Radiocarbon Dates for Central and Southern Brazil," *American Antiquity*, XXX, 1 (1964), pp. 25–33.

[14] Wendell C. Bennett and Junius B. Bird, *Andean Culture History*, Handbook Series, no. 15 (New York: American Museum of Natural History, 1949), pp. 12, 13.

in South America. In Phase II, modern fauna appears associated with long-stemmed projectile points, bone points, and a variety of crudely flaked tools. In Phase III, points comparable to Lauricocha III appear along with evidence of use of the bolas. In Phase IV, points shift in style to short-bladed varieties with broad stems or concave bases, and in Phase V, the bow apparently replaces the spear. These point varieties are widespread over Patagonia and indicate a relatively uniform culture. Points comparable to those in Phase I and II have been found at El Inga, Ecuador, raising the possibility there may have been a widespread early hunting phase over the Montane region prior to Lauricocha I.

Summary

Man was definitely in the New World, both North and South America, by 10,000 B.C. On the basis of geographical, linguistic, biological, and archaeological evidence, he migrated from Siberia in two waves. The first migrations probably lasted a long time and occurred in at least three pulsations that brought first the ancestors of the Macro-Carib-Ge speakers, then in succession the Equatorial–Andean (Macro-Arawakan-Quechuan) and the Macro-Mayan into the New World. These events may have taken place between 20,000 and 40,000 years ago. Population flow southward was probably a slow, gradual process stimulated by the pressure of arrival of new groups, internal population growth, and changing climatic conditions. A second wave came much later, and arrived in two pulsations: the earliest, around 6500 B.C., brought the Na-Dene speakers, the second, dating approximately 4000 B.C., the Eskimo.

Between 10,000 and 5000 B.C. the various groups adapted to nearly all the complex varieties of environment that emerged following the retreat of the Wisconsin ice sheet. Adaptation to the Arctic coast occurred a millennium later. Subsequent development between 5000 and 1000 B.C. involved increasingly more effective utilization of the wild resources of the new continent. Some of these adaptations in the northern and southern peripheries lasted until Contact.

From 5000 to 2500 B.C. in Mesoamerica and the Central Andes, a new solution to cultural adaptation emerged that was to revolutionize the life of the immigrants: food production, or agriculture; its repercussions were ultimately registered over most of the New World. In the remaining five chapters the history of this development will be traced.

Four Agricultural
Evolution and Revolution

The advantages and consequences of food production over food collection may be summarized in the following manner:

Firstly, although food collection under unusually favorable conditions may permit permanent residence—and some groups that practice farming are seminomadic—it is nevertheless generally true that food collection requires seasonal population movement and that food production requires permanent residence. Most significantly, agriculture permits an enormous expansion of the geographical range of sedentary residence.

Secondly, many writers have noted that hunting and gathering populations tend to achieve densities far below what is theoretically possible with a completely systematic use of all resources. The reasons lie in the basic ecology of all animals. In hunting and gathering systems, even in the most productive environment there is a considerable range of food quantity from season to season and from year to year; populations tend to stabilize only at the minimal levels. Admittedly, losses due to insects, droughts, frost, or floods affect the production of crops, but the range of variation is much reduced when compared to wild-food collection. Aside from this, the total amount of food that can be produced in a given environment—even in that in which only a small percentage of land is cultivated—is enormously increased. The result is a great potential increase in population density. High densities may in many cases not be achieved, but this is a historical problem and does not negate the fact that the potential is there.

The third major effect of agriculture is that it reduces the amount of time needed by a population to achieve a food supply. This surplus time may be channeled in many directions: economic, social, political, and religious. The tribesman uses this time in cooperative activities with his peers, whereas the peasant may have his surplus time appropriated by a ruling class. In essence, this is the key difference between the two social and economic systems that we have defined as tribes and states.

In summary, the effects of food production were threefold: the development of sedentary residence, the increase of population, and the increase of surplus time.

General Considerations

In all agrarian societies, whether tribe, chiefdom, or preindustrial state, one or a few plants normally provide the bulk of the food for most of the population. Other crops and animal foods round out the nutritional complex, but the primary food, usually referred to as the *staple crop*, provides most of the caloric requirements. Plants utilized as staples are always those that have a high caloric yield per weight and per area cultivated, and nearly all are either grains or roots. In the Old World, grains included wheat and barley as staples in Southwest and Central Asia, North China, North Africa, and Europe, rice in Southern and Southeast Asia, and millet and sorghum in the African Savanna. Roots have served as staples in parts of Southeast Asia and Oceania (taro, yams, sweet potatoes), and in the tropical forest and park savannas of Africa (yams, cocoyams, and, in post-Contact times, sweet potatoes and manioc). Only one crop, which is not a seed or root, has served as a staple: the plantain in the Great Lakes region of East Africa.

The caloric yield of roots is lower per weight than grains (only 20–40%) but roots more than make up for this deficiency in their higher yield per unit of land sown (frequently from two to six times the weight of grain). Roots, however, contain little more than carbohydrates, and their use as a staple must be compensated by a heavy intake of animal proteins. Grains yield from three to twenty times as much protein per weight as roots, and only minor additions of animal proteins are needed to provide a well-balanced diet.

The combination of crops, basic tools for producing them, and techniques of soil and moisture conservation makes up what can be called an agricultural system. In another volume in this series Wolf has defined five types of agricultural systems. His description is quoted in full below.

> 1. *Long-term fallowing systems*, associated with clearing by fire and cultivation with the hoe. These systems are called *swidden systems*, after an English dialect word for "burned clearing." Fields are cleared by firing the vegetation cover—grass, bush, or forest; planted to the point of decreasing yields; and abandoned to regain their fertility for a stipulated

number of years. Then other plots are similarly opened up for cultivation, and reoccupied after the critical period of regeneration is past. Swidden systems are found in both the Old and the New World. As we shall see below, such systems have supported peasantry only under exceptional circumstances.

2. *Sectorial fallowing systems,* in which cultivable land is divided into two or more sectors which are planted for two to three years and then left to fallow for three or four. The dominant tool is the hoe or the digging stick. Such systems are also found in both the Old and the New World, for instance, in West Africa and highland Mexico.

3. *Short-term fallowing systems,* in which land cultivated for one or two years is reoccupied after a year of regeneration. The dominant tool is the plow, driven by draft animals. Such systems are usually associated with the cultivation of cereals and are primarily found in Europe and Central Asia. Hence they may also be called *Eurasian grainfarming.*

4. *Permanent cultivation,* associated with techniques for assuring a *permanent water supply* for the growing crops. Such systems have been called *hydraulic systems* because they depend upon the construction of waterworks. They occur in the dry lands of both the New and the Old World where rivers can be tapped for irrigation, and in the tropical areas of the Old World where cultivators have succeeded in substituting a man-made landscape for the original forest cover and in tapping water resources to insure the production of their crops. There are no parallel systems in the tropical lowlands of the New World.

5. *Permanent cultivation of favored plots,* combined with a fringe of sporadically utilized hinterland. Such systems have been called *infield-outfield systems* where they occur along the Atlantic fringe of Western Europe. They are, however, also found in the Sudan, in highland Mexico, and elsewhere. The ability to cultivate permanently a given set of plots depends either upon special qualities of the soil, as in Atlantic Europe (where the limited areas of good soil on deltaic fans or fluvial and marine terraces are further supplemented by careful manuring), or upon the ability to irrigate permanently some portion of an otherwise unpromising landscape, as in parts of the Sudan and Mexico.[1]

New World Agriculture

In the Old World, agriculture was combined with a heavy emphasis on animal domestication. There was an intense symbiotic relationship between the two activities. Animals provided protein foods, skins, hair for textiles, fertilizers, hauled produce from farm to house to market, and were yoked to plows. Agriculture provided fodder for animals as well as crops for human consumption. This symbiosis was largely lacking in New World agriculture: cultivation was by human power alone, using a variety of hoe- and shovel-like tools made primarily of wood and stone. The only domestic animal found over most of the region was the dog; in Middle America and

[1] Eric R. Wolf, *Peasants* (Englewood Cliffs, N.J.: Prentice-Hall, Inc., 1966), pp. 20–21.

the southwestern part of the United States the turkey was added, in lowland South America the Muscovy duck. The only region where animal domestication was important was the Central Andes, where llamas were bred for meat and as beasts of burden (but not used in plowing), alpacas for wool, and guinea pigs and ducks for food. It was only in the Central Andes where animal fertilizers were extensively used. In central Mexico human fertilizers were used.

The application of considerable time and energy, and repeated, often continuous, cultivation of individual parcels of land is generally referred to in anthropology as *intensive agriculture*. Most American Indians practiced various forms of swidden cultivation, or what may be termed *extensive agriculture*, in which individual parcels of land are cultivated for short periods and the amount of time and energy spent in cultivation is relatively low. Specialized techniques of cultivation such as floodwater and permanent irrigation, terracing, contour hoeing, and swamp reclamation provided the basis for a more efficient use of the land in a few areas.

At the time of European Contact, the American Indian cultivated an impressive list of plants (approximately 120 species). Three of these crops served as staples: two were roots (manioc and white potatoes) and one a grain (maize). Maize was the staple throughout North America wherever agriculture was practicable—in the Intermediate area and on the Pacific coast of the Central Andes. In the Andean highlands white potatoes were the staple, particularly in areas above 3400 m. In the Amazon-Orinoco Basin, the Gran Chaco, and West Indies, manioc was the staple. Among many American Indians, other crops frequently served as co-staples. For example, several varieties of amaranth served as co-staples in the Mesoamerican and Andean highlands; maize was a co-staple in the Central Andes highlands in niches below 3600 m., while manioc and sweet potatoes were co-staples in the tropical lowlands of Mesoamerica and the Intermediate area.

Origins of New World Agriculture— Botanical Considerations

When we consider the possibilities for the origins of New World agriculture, keeping in mind the long list of plants domesticated, a variety of hypotheses might be reasonably suggested:

1. All New World cultigens were of Old World origin and were introduced fully domesticated by the immigrants.
2. Agricultural groups migrated from the Old to the New World, settled, and introduced a number of crops. They then either expanded their crop complex by experimentation with native flora or stimulated the native population to do so.
3. Agriculture in the New World was independent of, and parallel to, that of the Old World, and all plants found among the Indians at Contact were derived from native wild plants.
4. Although agriculture in the New World was basically an independent development, with most plants being native in origin, at a later date single or multiple migrations of Old World farmers introduced additional crops.

The first possibility is readily eliminated by an examination of botanical evidence. Most New World plants were not only unknown to Old World peoples at Contact but belong to genera not found in the wild state outside the New World. The second possibility is conceivable, but there are a number of theoretical difficulties involved in this hypothesis. If immigrants arrived with a fully evolved crop complex, it seems rather unlikely that they would waste much time experimenting with wild plants (at least as staple foods) of low caloric yields (wild maize, for example, produces only as much food in the entire ear as some modern domestic maize produces in each seed), and it would seem likelier that the natives would adopt the more productive, fully domesticated foreign plants.

Of the crops cultivated by the native Americans, only sweet potatoes, cotton, and the bottle gourds were surely found in both the New and Old worlds prior to 1492. The sweet potato provides the most convincing evidence of prehispanic interchange of domestic plants; it was found all over Polynesia by the earliest European explorers, and Maori oral tradition would date its arrival in New Zealand as early as 1000 A.D. Botanically, it is definitely a New World plant and apparently was carried by man from the New World to the Pacific islands. The case of the bottle gourd is not necessarily proof of migrant farmers; it is certainly an Old World plant, but it occurs in the New World in an archaeological context as early as 7000–5000 B.C. in Mexico, much too early for transpacific or transatlantic migrations. The gourd apparently will float in seawater for months without losing its power to germinate, so it may have colonized the New World as a wild or domestic plant without human assistance. The third plant, cotton, presents a more complex picture. Old World wild and domestic cotton has 13 large chromosomes; New World wild cotton has 13 small chromosomes. American-cultivated and Hawaiian wild cotton has 13 large and 13 small chromosomes. It has been argued, therefore, that cotton was first domesticated in the Old World, then introduced into the New World and hybridized with wild New World cotton, thus producing domestic New World cotton. It is further suggested that the hybrid was introduced into Hawaii where, for some undisclosed reason, its cultivation was abandoned, causing it to revert to a wild state. This reconstruction seems enormously complicated and invokes the idea of multiple population movements across enormous expanses of water. Several botanists have made a simpler suggestion: there was a native New World wild cotton with 13 large chromosomes that has since become extinct!

When we consider the great number of domestic plants that are of definite New World origin, the enormous geographic range of New World agriculture, and the rarity of foreign plants in the list, the conclusion seems inescapable that there was a long period of parallel and independent evolution of plant domestication within the New World. This leaves us with problems of when, where, and how this indigenous evolution took place. Archaeologists have wavered between two ideas: a single origin, with subsequent diffusion to other areas, and domestication in a few separate regions, with consequent diffusion between those areas and to others. They have generally favored Mesoamerica and/or the Central Andes as the source or sources. This conclusion is based primarily on the fact that culture in those two areas was more elaborate than elsewhere, suggesting a longer history of agriculture and population growth.

⌐   They have also relied heavily on botanical arguments, although the opinions of botanists have been varied and often contradictory. All domestic plants are highly altered descendants of wild plants; in many cases the wild ancestors still survive in their original habitats. This is the strongest kind of botanical argument for identification of a domestic plant's place of origin, but in many cases the wild ancestors have become extinct. Another line of evidence frequently used is that of the number of domestic races found from region to region. Where the number is greatest, the argument runs, there has been a longer period of evolution. A third guide is found in the ecological tolerance and preferences of the domestic plant.

There are a number of problems inherent in the last two approaches. A plant could first have been domesticated in a relatively homogeneous environment and later introduced into a microgeographically complex one. This ecological situation could have consequently stimulated a rapid evolution of many varieties. With respect to the third argument, domestication alters considerably, through selection, the adaptability of a plant.

Sauer [2] has emphasized a division of New World agricultural traditions into two basic types with respect to techniques and crops utilized as staples: seed cultivation and vegetative cultivation. In the former, seeds are used for sowing, and the focus of the crop complex is on seed crops like maize, various legumes, and cucurbits (some of the earliest squashes were cultivated for their seeds). The objective of the seed cultivator was to achieve a balanced nutritional system based almost entirely on plant foods. In vegetative cultivation, portions of roots or stems are planted in place of seeds, and the focus is on root crops like manioc, sweet potatoes, and white potatoes—the first two found in lower elevations, the last in higher ones. Historically, the pattern is a South American one. Sauer argues root crops were first cultivated by groups living along the coast or rivers of the Caribbean lowlands, where wild-animal proteins were so abundant that the objective of the cultivator was not to secure a balanced nutritional complex of plants but to secure a productive source of calories. In this connection, it is interesting to note that the Indians of the high Andes, where river resources are poor, domesticated more animals than any other group and developed several grain co-staples. Viewing Sauer's argument from a total historical perspective, one has the impression that the seed cultivation pattern was spatially a more viable one and had greater demographic potential since it freed the population from dependence on wild foods. As shall be demonstrated, this is supported by archaeological data.

On the basis of the number of species of crops, the number of races within species, and their geographical distribution, there were probably three hearth areas of New World plant domestication. We suspect that the evolution of agriculture in these three areas was essentially a parallel and separate development. One is the Mesoamerican highlands, the major hearth of Sauer's seed-crop tradition; the second area includes the high valleys and plateaus of the Central Andes, and the third the Caribbean lowlands of South America. Sauer's vegetative planting tradition may be divided, therefore, into two historically separate developments, lowland and highland. Each

[2] Carl O. Sauer, "Age and Area of American Cultivated Plants," *Proceedings*, 33rd International Congress of Americanists, vol. 1 (San Jose, Costa Rica, 1959), pp. 215–229.

of the three regions was probably the place of domestication for each of the three American Indian staples of maize, white potatoes, and manioc, and each produced a number of productive co-staples as well.

It is probable that there was borrowing of plants among the three centers; the overlapping distribution of cultigens obviously testifies to this. Plant domestication in general in the three areas, however, was not the product of direct or stimulus diffusion from the other centers. Cases of borrowing are, of course, of considerable interest since diffusion of plants is one of the best clues to population movement and cultural diffusion in general. There are difficulties, however, in the use of such data. Archaeologists should be warned against too facile an argument for diffusion on the basis of distribution of domestic plants. For example, in the case of the Central Andean and Mesoamerican hearths, approximately half the cultivated species in one area were found in the other in the 16th century. The list includes maize, several beans (Indian runner, lima, common, jack), cucurbits (moschata, tzilacayote, lagenaria), roots (peanuts, sweet manioc, sweet potato), fruits (two types of peppers, anona, sweet sop, pineapple, avocado, papaya, guava, cacao), two species of tobacco, and the calabash tree. Several of these may have diffused from the Caribbean hearth to both areas, so correspondences in the lists may not be the product of direct contact between Mesoamerica and the Central Andes. An even thornier problem derives from our lack of information on distribution of wild ancestors of any plant in the above list—they could have been distributed over the entire region from Mexico to Peru and have undergone separate and multiple domestication.

In fact, the domestication of maize, distribution of which in historic times has been used as a strong argument for interareal diffusion, may present such a case. Wellhausen [3] studied races of maize found today in Mexico and grouped them into ten races, four of which, all popcorns of relatively low yield, he calls *ancient indigenous races*. Four others are exotic races believed to be of South American, probably Colombian, origin. As the product of hybridization, first among the four indigenous races, combined with constant recrossing with tripsicum (a wild relative of maize), and later with exotic South American races, much-higher-yielding, more productive hybrid races developed in late prehistoric times (archeological data suggest the Classic and Postclassic periods). It is conceivable that maize had a single origin in Mesoamerica and was diffused to South America, where new races were evolved that were then reintroduced into Mesoamerica; but a less complicated explanation would be one demonstrating separate evolution in the two areas followed by later interchange of evolved domestic races.

Archaeological Evidence—
The Mesoamerican Hearth

The most detailed data on evolution of New World agriculture are those gathered by MacNeish in the Tehuacán Valley in central Mexico.[4]

[3] E. J. Wellhausen, *Races of Maize in Central America*, National Academy of Science, National Research Council Publication 511 (1957).

[4] Richard S. MacNeish, "Ancient Mesoamerican Civilization," *Science*, vol. 143 (1964), pp. 531–537.

The valley floor is 1500 m above sea level and has an average annual rainfall of 300–600 mm and a xerophytic vegetation; the climate is arid enough to permit preservation of plant remains. On the basis of excavations in a number of caves and open sites, MacNeish has defined a long sequence of cultures that reflect the process of shift from hunting and gathering to sedentary village subsistence.

The earliest phase is called *Ajuerreado* and dates from 10,000 to 7200 B.C. The culture was comparable to that of Montane Hunters and Gatherers of the Old Cordilleran complex. The subsequent *El Riego* phase (7200–5200 B.C.) witnessed a shift in direction to the Desert tradition. Plant food became of increasing significance. Along with chipped stone tools comparable to those of the *Ajuerreado* phase, a greater variety of ground stone milling stones appear, suggesting a focus on wild seeds. The settlement pattern included two types of campsites: microbands during dry seasons, shifting to macrobands—consisting of several families—during rainy seasons, when plant foods were abundant. Among plants collected were several that later became cultigens: squash, chile peppers, and avocados, suggesting incipient cultivation.

Several innovations occur in the succeeding *Coxcatlán* phase (5200–3400 B.C.). Macroband campsites were larger and apparently occupied for a longer period, both of which features imply a new technique of food collection. In the refuse were found a much greater number of plants that were to be future cultigens: maize, chile peppers, avocados, gourds, tepary beans, several varieties of zapotes, three species of squash, jack beans, possibly the common bean, and cotton. It seems certain that some of these were already cultigens. The maize, however, has been classified by Manglesdorf as wild maize.

In the succeeding *Abejas* phase (3400–2300 B.C.) evidence of incipient cultivation of maize is incontrovertible. Maize cobs are much more variable in size, and the larger ones are several times the size of Coxcatlán wild maize. Furthermore, portions of leaves and stems indicate that the plant was well on its way toward its evolved form. Abejas maize is clearly a descendant of the native wild plant. Wild maize continued to be collected during the phase, at the end of which a new variety of domestic maize with tripsicum introgression appeared that hybridized with, and ultimately replaced, the native variety. Since tripsicum does not grow in the Tehuacán Valley, the new maize must have come from elsewhere; Manglesdorf suggests the Balsas Valley in central Mexico.

The significance of this new level of incipient domestication is reflected by a shift of macroband residence to river terraces, where more suitable conditions for agriculture were found. There is some evidence of year-round residence in some macroband settlements, and pit houses of substantial construction appear. Macroband camps consisted of five to ten pit houses; nevertheless, MacNeish argues from feces analysis that only 30% of the food was derived from domestic plants. The ecological system may have been comparable to that of the historic acorn gatherers of California, with sedentary villages and outlying campsites; in this case, domestic plants rather than acorns provided the anchor. Technological innovations include hemispherical and flatbottom stone bowls and tecomates (neckless jars), and the first appearance of the Mesoamerican obsidian—cylindrical core—blade tradition.

In the succeeding *Purrón* phase (2300–1500 B.C.) crude, poorly-fired, crumbly pottery appeared with forms in direct imitation of stone vessels, suggesting a local invention. By 1500 B.C., sedentary village life and a primary dependence on agriculture were fully developed. The introduction of tripsicoid maize demonstrates that agriculture was not a unique invention of the population of the Tehuacán Valley and that similar experiments in plant domestication were taking place elsewhere. MacNeish's earlier excavations in Tamaulipas on the northeastern frontier of Mesoamerica point in the same direction. A long sequence of occupations in dry caves in that area reveal a closely parallel sequence of changes in technology, subsistence, and settlement patterns, with some variation. Between 7000 and 5000 B.C. gourds, two species of peppers, and one species of squash appear as domestic plants, followed between 5000 and 3000 B.C. by the common bean and between 3000 and 2200 B.C. by a fully-domesticated maize of a different type from that in Tehuacán but apparently not of local origin. One of the Tehuacán squashes (moschata) does not appear until 1800 B.C. in Tamaulipas. The implication of the data is that plant domestication was not so much an invention as an ecological process taking place simultaneously over much of the arid Mesoamerican highlands.

Archaeological Evidence— The Central Andean Hearth

Information on the evolution of agriculture in the Central Andean hearth is still scanty. Nearly all research has focused on the desert coast because of excellent preservation of vegetal remains. This is unfortunate, since it is doubtful whether any of the Central Andean cultigens originated in that area. The deficiency of research is particularly aggravated by the fact that the complex of highland grains and root crops was not much used by coastal peoples, yet domestication of these crops is the key to the history of plant domestication generally in the Central Andes.

Marine resources off the coast of Peru are extraordinarily rich, a product of the cold Humboldt current. Particularly abundant are sea lions, manatees, killer whales, shorebirds, shellfish, and fish. The Peruvian coast is therefore an ideal habitat for littoral-oriented gatherers, and we have evidence that such a pattern was well established by 5000 B.C. Unlike other littoral traditions discussed previously, there is evidence of incipient cultivation from the beginning of the pattern.

On the basis of excavations by Bird,[5] Lanning,[6] and Engel,[7] early development of agriculture on the Peruvian coast has been organized in two phases: pre-Cotton, ranging in date from 3600 to 2500 B.C., and post-Cotton, which begins around 2500 B.C. and ends with the appearance of pottery in all coastal valleys around 1200 B.C.

Evidence of the earliest phase is limited to the South and Central Coast.

---

[5] Junius B. Bird, "Preceramic Cultures in Chicama and Viru," in *A Reappraisal of Peruvian Archaeology*, ed., Wendell C. Bennett, Memoirs of the Society for American Archaeology, no. 4 (Menasha, Wisc., 1948), pp. 21–28.

[6] Edward P. Lanning, "Early Man in Peru," *Scientific American*, CCXIII, 4 (1965), pp. 68–76.

[7] Frederic Engel, *A Preceramic Settlement on the Central Coast of Peru: Asia, Unit 1*, Transactions of the American Philosophical Society, LIII, part 3 (1963).

Fullest documentation is from sites in the Ancón and Chilca valleys, both waterless today. The site of Chilca is found on the edge of a coastal terrace and consists of a series of interlocking refuse mounds, each consisting of beds of earth, shell, and other cultural debris associated with earth house floors. Houses had frames constructed of bundles of cane with a grass cover. Evidence indicates a permanent settlement of perhaps 100 families.

Subsistence included sea resources, and both wild and cultivated plants. Mollusks, crabs, fish bones, shorebird bones, turtle bones, and particularly sea lion bones were abundant. Wild-plant remains, particularly tubers, were found as well as domesticated lima beans, jack beans, gourds, and squash. Engel suggests that agriculture was of the floodwater type. Seasonal rains in the mountains produced annual floods in the Chilca Quebadra, and the moist soils were used for cultivation, a pattern comparable to that of historic Yumans of the U.S. Southwest.

Lanning reports a comparable phase from the Ancón Valley. During the final phase of occupation of the lomas by highland hunters and gatherers, a new cultural complex appeared on the Ancón beach. The site consists of a shell midden, and subsistence was a combination of shellfish gathering and squash cultivation. Lanning argues that the population were newcomers, unrelated to the old Lomas Hunters.

The post-Cotton phase is reported from numerous sites from Chicama to Nazca. Sites on the North Coast consist of large shell middens. Between Casma and Nazca, however, sites are larger, and some have extensive residential areas with associated monumental architecture. Most sites, whatever their size, are situated near the beach, and so subsistence continued to be a combination of cultivation and use of littoral resources. The number of cultigens had expanded enormously since the early phase and included chile peppers, two species of squash, lima beans, jack beans, lucuma, achira, guava, jicama, and cotton. The last was used for twined cloth, nets, and bags. None of the crops on the list was among the historic staples and co-staples; agriculture remained a secondary resource. The location of sites along the beach also points to a secondary role for cultivation. Lanning reports one exception in the Chillón Valley, where he found remains of a littoral-incipiently agricultural community in which white potatoes and sweet potatoes were both present. He argues that the population were highlanders who had migrated to the coast.

Pottery appears between 1200 and 1400 B.C. on the Peruvian coast and is apparently considerably younger than in Mesoamerica and the Intermediate area. Within a century or two of this event, maize, sweet manioc, and avocado were added to the crop complex. Two varieties of maize were apparently involved: one small-eared race of low productivity was introduced first and had little immediate effect on the subsistence patterns. It was followed by a much more productive variety between 900 and 800 B.C. that revolutionized the life of the coastal peoples.[8]

Many writers have suggested that maize was introduced by immigrants from Mesoamerica; however, early maize from the South Coast is not a

---

[8] In his recent book, *Peru before the Incas* (Englewood Cliffs, N.J.: Prentice-Hall, Inc., 1967), Lanning now argues that pottery on the North and Central Coast appears by 1800 B.C. and that the earlier type of maize was present a century or two prior to this date.

Mesoamerican type, but is instead related to a historic Andean highland race. There is a strong possibility that maize was separately domesticated in the highlands. Regardless of the history of maize, the appearance of monumental architecture at Kotosh (see Chapter Five) by 1800 B.C. and evidence of sedentary village life by 1000 B.C. all over the highland province convincingly argue for great time depth to agriculture in that region.

Archaeological Evidence—
The Caribbean Hearth

For the third postulated agricultural hearth, that of the Tropical Lowlands, we have virtually no data. We do not know when, where, or how the first steps toward domestication of tropical root crops were taken. Sauer has argued that it was an independent process from that of seed cultivation and occurred earlier as well; he favors the Caribbean lowlands as the source.

Another possibility is an origin in lowland Mesoamerica, following and perhaps stimulated by experiments in seed cultivation in the neighboring highlands. Archaeological data cannot presently resolve this controversy. In Mesoamerica sedentary village life based on agriculture was present in the tropical lowlands of the South Gulf Coast as early as 1500 B.C., but whether this was the product of local evolution based on root crops or the introduction of grain crops from the neighboring highlands is not known. Data from Ecuador suggest that coastal groups lacked agriculture until maize was introduced either by sea from Mesoamerica or from the neighboring Andean highlands, some time between 1500 and 1000 B.C. In Colombia and Venezuela—Sauer's suggested hearth for American tropical roots crops—pottery griddles for manioc cakes appear in the local ceramic sequence around 1000 B.C. Sweet manioc apparently appeared on the coast of Peru at approximately the same date. In all probability there was a lengthy period of use of manioc prior to the invention of manioc flour and griddle cakes. It is possible that early ceramic sites in Colombia such as Puerto Hormiga and Barlovento combined littoral gathering with incipient cultivation of root crops comparable to the Peruvian coastal pattern.

In summary, archaeological data support the native origin of New World agriculture as a whole and also of multiple centers of domestication, not only within the New World, but within culture areas.

Five Tribes, Chiefdoms, and States in Mesoamerica

When Cortez arrived in 1519 he found Mesoamerica occupied by a great number of ethnic groups with highly distinctive cultures and speaking different, often unrelated languages. One characteristic feature of Mesoamerican civilization throughout its history was intense regionalism; horizon styles emerged periodically, but they interrupted only temporarily and briefly this basic pattern of regional diversity. On the Gulf coastal plain and neighboring escarpment were three distinctive groups, Huastec, Totonac, and Olmec; the Central Mexican Plateau and adjacent southern escarpment were occupied by Otomi and Nahua speakers (among the latter, the politically dominant Aztec). The highlands and Pacific coasts of Oaxaca, eastern Guerrero, and southern Puebla were occupied by Mixtec and Zapotec; west of the Aztec in the highlands of Michoacán were Tarascans, and various groups of the Maya language family occupied the Yucatan peninsula and the highlands and Pacific coast of Guatemala. The balance of Mesoamerica was occupied by less highly developed groups, some of which continued to remain on a chiefdom societal level as late as 1519. All of these groups, although individually varying, shared in one great cultural tradition that archaeologists refer to as Mesoamerican.[1]

The basis of this tradition was a highly developed agriculture characterized by a great number of crops, but with maize as the staple. Animal domestication was incipiently developed and land transportation therefore unelaborated. Metallurgy (gold, silver, copper) was used primarily for ornaments for the ruling class and in the religious cult. Most basic cutting tools were stone: chipped obsidian for scrapers, knives, projectile points, and drills; ground stone for tools for woodworking and the grinding of grain. The technological stage was what archaeologists call Neolithic. Many crafts were extraordinarily highly developed: weaving (cotton and maguey); ceramics (pottery and figurines); monumental stone sculpture; feather mosaic; lapidary work using jade, turquoise and other semiprecious stones; and, finally, architecture. This last involved high, terraced platforms with stairways ascending to summit temples or low platforms for elite residences, each built of earth and stone, with lime concrete mortar and lime plaster surfacing. Economically there was a great deal of specialization: community and part-time, professional and full-time. Goods were distributed through elaborate market systems by organized caravans of human packtrains.

All over Mesoamerica people were organized in little states with populations of tens of thousands of people, ruled by petty kings or in some cases, by orders of priests. Such states were in constant military competition. Superstates enjoyed brief periods of prosperity based on conquest and tribute-collecting. Society was stratified in two basic levels: a landed nobility with control of production and distribution of goods via markets and taxation, and a peasant class that provided labor for war, construction, and cultivation of land, along with agricultural products and craft products, to support the nobility. In many areas this system of social stratification was more elaborate, with professional warriors, elite craftsmen, serfs, and slaves as clearly defined social classes.

The constant, recurrent, and dominating theme of Mesoamerican civilization, however, was clearly religion. Much of the fine craftsmanship and architectural energy was devoted to the gods. The religious system involved a pantheon with specialized functions, the universally important deities being agricultural, especially the rain gods. The gods were omnipotent and had to be propitiated for there to exist any stable relationship between man and his world. This idea reached its climax in human sacrifice. Temples were built as homes of the gods; a calendar was invented to predict the seasons and the behavior of the gods and to regulate the elaborate ceremonial that was dedicated to them. A professional priesthood with formal schools for novices

---

[1] The following works provide a useful general introduction to the subject matter contained in this chapter: Michael D. Coe, *Mexico* and *The Maya* (New York: Frederick A. Praeger, Inc., 1962, 1966); Miguel Covarrubias, *Indian Art of Mexico and Central America* (New York: Alfred A. Knopf, Inc., 1957); Sylvanus G. Morley, *The Ancient Maya*, 3rd ed. (Palo Alto: Stanford University Press, 1956); Bernardino Sahagun, *Florentine Codex: General History of the Things of New Spain*, Parts I-XII, ed. and trans., Arthur J. O. Anderson and Charles Dibble (Santa Fe: The School of American Research and the University of Utah, 1951–1963); John E. S. Thompson, *The Rise and Fall of Maya Civilization* (Norman, Okla.: University of Oklahoma Press, 1954); and George C. Vaillant, *The Aztecs of Mexico* (New York: Doubleday & Company, Inc., 1962).

and an elaborate rank system administered the cult. Intellectual development included refined systems of astrology and writing.

Within this basic pattern of cultural uniformity was an extraordinary diversification of regional subcultures and at least two fundamentally dissimilar patterns. One was in the tropical lowlands and involved swidden agriculture, lower population density, smaller development of markets and craft specialization (other than elite crafts), greater focus on religion, less military development, and lack of evolution of large states and true cities. The settlement pattern included two types of communities: ceremonial precincts where priests and elite craftsmen resided, and hamlets, in which lived the peasants who made up most of the population. In the highlands, or at least the arid highlands, agriculture was more intensive, involving irrigation and terracing, and there was a denser population per unit of agricultural land. Markets, as well as community and occupational specialization, were much more highly developed, involving even the peasant crafts. The status system had less religious emphasis: there were professional warriors and a secular nobility. Warfare generally was more elaborated and of greater economic significance, and there was a marked tendency toward the formation of huge tributary states. The most striking characteristic of the arid highland cultures, however, was the presence of urban centers.

Formative Tribes and Chiefdoms

In Chapter Four we summarized the steps by which man, in this area, changed from nomadic hunter and gatherer to sedentary farmer, from resident of camp to that of village, from membership in bands to one of tribe. During the period from 2300 B.C. to A.D. 1, Mesoamerican society evolved from tribes to chiefdoms. This long period of time is referred to as the Formative, and it may be divided into three phases based on the appearance and diffusion, first, of the basic village level of Mesoamerican culture (including such traits as primary dependence on agriculture, ceramics, permanent villages of substantial houses, and a complex of chipped and ground stone tools), then of the elite level, including monumental architecture and sophisticated art, the two combined in civic–religious centers. The appearance of the latter initiates the social differentiation between center and satellite that was to be a distinctive feature of this civilization. In the Early Formative phase (2300–1500 B.C.) the village level became established in the Central Plateau. In Middle Formative times (1500–500 B.C.) the elite level emerged in a restricted region in the Central Highlands and adjacent South Gulf Coast, and in the Late Formative (500 B.C.–A.D. 1) this elite level became firmly established over most of the culture area.

Archaeological evidence of the Early Formative and first three centuries of the Middle Formative is limited to the Tehuacán Valley (Purrón and Early Ajalpan). In all probability, later research will reveal evidence of a wider distribution in the Central Plateau and the Balsas River Basin. In the Tehuacán Valley the relatively simple Purrón ceramic complex evolved into the much more elaborate ceramics of the Early Ajalpan subphase (1500–1200 B.C.). The basic forms of tecomate (neckless jar), hemispherical bowl, and flatbottom bowl persist, but the ware is technically better and decorated by zoned-brushing, punctation, and incision. Also present are simple painting, consisting of red bands on the rims, and small, solid, handmade pottery figurines, the beginnings of a distinctive Mesoamerican artistic tradition. Sites consist of sedentary villages of wattle and daub houses, with populations estimated between 100 and 300 inhabitants.

In the above discussion the South Gulf Coast has not been mentioned. By 1200 B.C. a relatively complex chiefdom had become established at San Lorenzo Tenochtitlán. This would imply, first, the presence of smaller, less complex chiefdoms in the general region a few centuries earlier, and second, that sedentary villages were present in the area during the Early Formative. We have therefore initiated the Middle Formative at 1500 B.C.

Between 1200 and 500 B.C., the South Gulf Coast was the scene of a spectacular cultural tradition in which a simple sedentary village life was transformed into the first elaborate culture in Mesoamerica. Major centers, aside from San Lorenzo, were found at La Venta and Tres Zapotes. The specific culture has been referred to as Olmec after the historical occupants of the region. Centers were composed of high, truncated, sloping-sided rectangular mounds; low, elongated platforms; and small, conical mounds. All were constructed of earth and grouped into plaza complexes. At La Venta was a sacred enclosure composed of a picket fence of basalt columns imbedded in low earth platforms. A conical mound delimited one side of the enclosure, and within it was a tomb constructed of basalt logs. There is a possibility that many Olmec mounds had a primarily funerary function, since evidence of summit temples or stairways on even the largest mounds is absent.

Middle Formative Olmecs were also master sculptors. Associated with buildings are basalt sculptures of monumental size, human heads carved in the round, and relief carving on sarcophagi, stelae, and flattopped altars. They also manufactured great numbers of smaller objects in various types of fine-grained stone (jade, jadeite, and serpentine), beautifully polished figurines, masks, celts, and ornaments.

Olmec art represents primarily religious themes, and is a pictorial cosmology. The Olmecs believed in a mythical union of a male jaguar and a woman that produced a race of hybrid rain gods, usually portrayed with combinations of feline and infantile features in a highly distinctive style. Other sculptures represent humans, possibly chiefs or priests. Extensive excavations at La Venta have failed to reveal large residential areas, and the site was a ceremonial center occupied by a chiefly lineage with most of the population dispersed in hamlets or neighborhoods.

Portable Olmec carvings have been found widely distributed in the Mesoamerican highlands as trade objects. They are particularly abundant in the Upper Balsas Basin and occur frequently as offerings in high-status burials associated with a great variety of ceramic objects that include vessels, figurines, masks, and helmets. In some cases the Olmec jaguar–infant is modeled or incised, but other designs portray a variety of supernatural beings—a spirit of duality with two faces, heads, or bodies; a hunchback dwarf; an obese creature; a variety of masked figures; "Pretty Ladies"; and "Baby Faces"— rare or absent in the art of La Venta.

Highland sites are primarily large villages with associated cemeteries. Two, Chalcatzingo and Totimehuacán, have earth mounds, but monumental sculpture, except for cliff relief carvings, is absent. The evidence suggests that portions of the neighboring plateau were scenes of a distinctive religious tradition, heavily influenced by the Gulf Coast Olmec during the Middle Formative. Evidence of status tombs with elaborate offerings (in some cases with accompanying human sacrifices) indicate a chiefdom social structure, and the size of centers suggests that they were smaller than those on the Gulf Coast. Sanders has referred to this distinctive regional culture as *Amacusac*.[2]

Olmec portable objects are found widely distributed outside the Olmec–Amacusac heartland. Trade routes were apparently extensive at this time, and much of Olmec influence in the Amacusac and other regions was probably the product of trade. Coe has suggested that the search for jade was the major stimulus for the establishment of this trade.[3] There is evidence that some tenets of Olmec religion were diffused as well, particularly the concept of a felinized rain god. In all probability, by the close of the Early Formative, perhaps earlier, agriculture had diffused over most of Mesoamerica. During the Middle Formative sedentary villages were sprinkled from Salvador to Central Mexico and many, but not all, participated in this trade network. Most remained tribally organized throughout the phase, and chiefdoms seem to have been limited to the South Gulf Coast, Central Plateau, Balsas Basin, and Oaxaca Highlands. Some ceramic traits diffused through the network as well: there are striking similarities in pottery from such widely spaced areas as the Guatemala Coast, the Central Valley of Chiapas, and the Gulf Coast. Ceramics as a craft probably did not derive from a common source, since stylistic divergences are striking as well.

The Late Formative phase witnessed the achievement of a chiefdom social level over nearly all of central and southern Mesoamerica and the emergence of the initial phases of the various Classic regional civilizations. It is also the first time that we have definite evidence of the typical Mesoamerican temple pyramid. During Late Formative times the platform was faced with clay or dressed stone and constructed of earth, or of earth combined with stone. By the end of the period, the surface was plastered with slaked lime and the basic religious architectural form was complete. Also making their appearance for the first time were writing and the calendar. In all probability this was the phase in which Mesoamerican society evolved from chiefdoms to states in some regions. Major chiefdoms or incipient states were found at Kaminaljuyú, in highland Guatemala, Izapa on the Chiapas coast, Chiapa de Corzo in the Central Valley of Chiapas, Monte Albán in Oaxaca, Cuicuilo on the Central Mexican Plateau, Tres Zapotes and Cerro de Las Mesas on the Gulf Coast, and Tikal in the Maya Lowlands.

Various types of swidden cultivation were probably in vogue during most of the Formative. For Late Formative times there is a growing body of evidence indicating that more intensive practices were emerging, including irrigation and terracing, in the drier upland regions. We suspect that they may have begun even earlier in the Upper Balsas Valley.

---

[2] William T. Sanders and Barbara J. Price, *Mesoamerica: The Evolution of a Civilization* (New York: Random House, Inc., 1968), p. 119.

[3] Coe, *Mexico*, p. 86.

The Classic and Postclassic
in Mesoamerican History

During the Classic Period, Mesoamerican civilization reached spectacular heights. Many archaeologists consider the period one of culture climax and see the succeeding Postclassic as a period of decline. This evaluation is based primarily on the profile of history of art for the Lowland Maya area. The Maya reached the peak of their development in architecture, sculpture, painting, stucco, and clay-modeling during the Classic. Beginning around A.D. 300 they began to erect, at periodic intervals, carved stelae with commemorative dates; the custom was abandoned shortly after A.D. 900 and the term Classic normally applies to the period, from A.D. 300 to 900, during which they followed this tradition. The phase between the end of the Formative (A.D. 1) and A.D. 300 is referred to as Protoclassic. Here we have appended it to the Classic.

Several other contemporary regional cultures reached comparable developments in the major Mesoamerican arts during the period, particularly Monte Albán, Tajín on the Central Gulf Coast, and Teotihuacán in Central Mexico. The succeeding Postclassic in some areas witnessed an artistic decline comparable to that of the Lowland Maya. The end of the Classic, in the view of many archaeologists, was marked by abandonment of numerous major centers and by wholesale population movements, including barbarian invasions from the north.

The Classic Period has been characterized as one of peaceful coexistence, widespread trade, theocratic government, and absence of urbanism and large states based on conquest. The succeeding Postclassic has been characterized by militarism, large empires based on conquest, secular government, the decline of religion and religious art, and the development of cities. This contrast was based essentially on comparison of Classic Maya with Postclassic Aztec, two groups residing in areas 600 km apart and in strikingly different environments.

Recent studies tend to challenge this picture. In many areas the Postclassic did not witness a period of artistic decline; the great Classic centers were in fact abandoned over a period of 600 years, not all at once in a great cataclysm; and militarism, urbanism, and imperialistic states were all present during the Classic. The supposed cultural differences between Classic and Postclassic actually reflect differences in regional culture and are related to ecological factors. On page 53 we stressed the presence of two ecosystems in Mesoamerica, a highland and a lowland. This differentiation emerged during Late Formative times and became pronounced in the Classic. In the following pages we will discuss in detail two Classic civilizations representing this contrast, Teotihuacán and the Lowland Maya.

We have characterized even the most complex Formative cultures as chiefdoms. Some archaeologists would probably argue that they were states. We disagree, and believe that the Classic centers represented a new plateau of societal evolution. Many were of huge size, their architecture was both more massive and more skillful than that of any Formative site, and, as impressive as were some of the Formative crafts, they were not comparable, quantitatively or qualitatively, to those of the Classic. Finally, there is conclusive evidence of much larger and more complex political organizations in the later periods.

The Urban Revolution
in Central Mexico

Teotihuacán is an enormous site situated in the largest, most productive topographic unit in the Mesoamerican highlands. The floor of the Basin of Mexico, as it is called, lies 2240 m above sea level and its mountain walls ascend to nearly 6000 m in the southeast. The basin has a surface area of approximately 8000 sq. km. Annual rainfall varies from 1200 mm on the southern slopes to less than 500 mm in the north. Rainfall, and therefore most drainage, is seasonal and collects into a chain of interconnected lakes. There are a number of permanent streams fed by meltwater from mountain glaciers and subterranean drainage. Teotihuacán is situated immediately above a concentration of 80 springs.

The size of the site, evidence of continuously dense occupational remains on the surface, and evidence from excavations all demonstrate that it was an urban center. Recent surveys by Millon indicate that the city covered 20 sq. km, included 4000 residences—most of these apartment houses—and had a population of from 50,000 to 100,000 inhabitants.[4] As in most cities, the growth of Teotihuacán witnessed continuous conflict between amorphous accretion and the need for order. The city went through a number of phases of rebuilding, and the idea of a formal grid (57 m square) of streets and houses was early conceived by the city architects and was imposed in a series of urban renewal plans that ultimately involved at least the central 12 to 15 sq. km.

Teotihuacán was oriented on two axes that consisted of two wide avenues, each between six and eight km long. They met at a huge architectural complex that served as the economic, religious, and administrative center of the city. The north–south avenue split the center into two huge, walled compounds. The west compound measured 400 by 600 m and apparently served as a market. The east compound, the Ciudadela, measured 400 m square and served as a combination temple and sacerdotal residence. There is evidence from Millon's plan that the Ciudadela was an inner structure within a truly gigantic complex of buildings that measured 800 × 600 m.

North of the civic center, and aligned with both sides of the north–south avenue were other important buildings of the city, elite residences, and temple complexes, of which the total number runs into the hundreds. Two temples, the Sun and the Moon, were among the largest structures ever created by American Indians. The terraced platform of the Sun Pyramid, for example, was 64 m high and measured 210 m square at the base. The scale of construction at Teotihuacán staggers the imagination, and the contrast between chiefdom and state can be convincingly demonstrated by scale alone. The entire civic center of LaVenta, the largest Middle Formative center, could easily be accommodated within the market at Teotihuacán! Even more

---

[4] René F. Millon, "Teotihuacán," *Scientific American*, CCXIV, 14, pp. 38–48.

convincing evidence of a new level of evolution of economic and political institutions is the nerve center of the city described above.

Besides being accompanied by monumental architecture in earth, stone, and lime, the growth of the state at Teotihuacán saw spectacular developments in mural painting, stone sculpture (both portable and monumental), weaving, featherwork, ceramics, and obsidian chipping—all done in a specific, unmistakable style.

Most of the residences at Teotihuacán consisted of multifamily houses, each occupying a city block. Each house may be described as a compound, fronting on narrow alleys. Access was carefully controlled by a restricted number of gates, each with a porter's room; the house consisted of a cluster of adjoining apartments grouped around a central court, altar, and shrine. The compound was equipped with an underground drain that communicated with the complex sewerage system of the city. The plan suggests that the residents of a compound were socially related, either by kin ties or by a patron–client relationship or both.

The distribution of artifacts on the surface and from excavation, the quality of the technology, and indications of mass production (use of figurine molds, for example) all point to a pattern of intensive craft specialization within the city. There is also evidence some city residents were farmers or part-time farmers–craftsmen. Differences in plan and quality of construction, in such architectural embellishments as mural painting, and in grave offerings indicate wide variations in wealth and political power in Teotihuacán society. In short, we have abundant and overwhelming proof that Teotihuacán was a city and that Teotihuacán society had reached the level defined by Service as the Ancient State.

This reconstruction is also supported by archaeological evidence from the immediate rural hinterland of Teotihuacán and from regions as far afield as the Guatemala Highlands and the Maya Lowlands. Artifacts and house-types of villages within the Basin of Mexico are identical with those from the city. The former were not made locally and were apparently purchased in the urban market. During the earliest phase of the history of Teotihuacán, rural settlements were dispersed into hamlets and neighborhoods. During later phases, populations of these dispersed settlements were gathered into large, compact, planned villages and towns, some of which had a civic center that closely imitated in plan that of the city. The data indicate the exercise of thorough economic and political control of the countryside by the urban government.

The Teotihuacán style in architecture and craft products was characteristic of much of the Central Plateau and Upper Balsas Basin. Many of the artifacts were manufactured in local urban centers, others brought from Teotihuacán. Close stylistic resemblances of the objects to those from Teotihuacán, in addition to the fact none of the local centers approximated that center in size, points to the conclusion that this region was a core state ruled from Teotihuacán. In the 6th century A.D. the Teotihuacán style diffused to Kaminaljuyú in Highland Guatemala, Tikal in the Maya Lowlands, and the South Gulf Coast. It occurs in the form of temples, portable objects placed in high-status tombs (particularly diagnostic are fresco painted vases with slab tripod feet), sculpture, and painting, the latter two in some cases representing Tláloc, the patron god of the city. Teotihuacán influence on regional arts and crafts, however, has been reported over virtually the entire central and southern portions of Mesoamerica. The conclusion seems inescapable that the city was the center of a great empire comparable to the historic Aztec.

We are still far from understanding the basic factors that produced the growth of the city and its political preeminence. The higher mountain basins of the plateau were clearly marginal, demographically and culturally, in Early and Middle Formative times. They are difficult environments for extensive cultivation, owing to a combination of low rainfall and winter frosts. The retardation or marginality may be due to this factor. Once the twin problem of frosts and droughts was resolved—and this was resolved in Aztec times by irrigation and terracing—the great size of the basins and their extensive areas of alluvial plain and gentle slopes converted them from marginal to nuclear areas. The Basin of Mexico in 1519 had a minimal population of one and one-half million inhabitants and a density of 200 persons per sq. km. Recent evidence indicates that an initial development of intensive agriculture occurred in Late Formative times and that expansion of the techniques of terracing and irrigation provided the base for the explosive growth of the city around the time of Christ.

Teotihuacán was apparently attacked and its power destroyed in the 7th century A.D. It continued to function as a provincial center, however, until the arrival of Cortez.

Civilization Without Cities— The Maya Lowlands

The extensive tropical lowlands that comprise the Yucatan peninsula, the adjacent foothills of the Guatemala Highlands, western Honduras, the alluvial plain of Tabasco, and the adjacent escarpment of the Chiapas Highlands were occupied, during the Classic Period, by groups who spoke various languages of the Maya linguistic stock. The style of peasant technology varied considerably from subarea to subarea, but on the elite level all groups participated in a Great Tradition that archaeologists refer to as Lowland Maya civilization. Hallmarks of this tradition include a specific and unique sculptural style, an epigraphic system, and architecture, diagnostic features of which are masonry buildings with corbelled roofs constructed of dressed stone and lime concrete. Lowland Maya sculpture, architecture, lapidary work (in jade, chert, and marble), painting, stucco and clay-modeling, textiles, and featherwork all represent climactic developments in New World culture.

The Maya habitat may be classified as tropical forest, varying in density from scrubby and xerophytic in northwestern Yucatan to rain forests in the south. There are variations in rainfall, topography, and hydrography, but everywhere the major problem faced by the Maya peasant was the lush and exuberant vegetation. This was resolved by a variety of swidden cultivation based on maize with root crops as co-staples. Today most swidden is practiced in areas of low population density where land is abundant and carefully organized cycling is unnecessary. As population density rises, increasing attention is paid to careful cycling until ultimately all land is in various stages of use and succession, and a stable cycling system becomes established. Conklin has referred to this stage of swidden cultivation as integral swidden.[5] Field studies suggest that the Maya Lowlands will support population densities of from 10 to 40 persons per sq. km and still maintain a stable swidden system.

The Maya may have colonized portions of the area as early as the Early Formative Period, but convincing evidence of occupation does not predate the Late Formative. A simple tribal society apparently functioned in the region until a century or two before Christ; between then and A.D. 300 there was a rapid population growth and the emergence of a chiefdom society. There is also convincing evidence of the arrival of groups from the neighboring highlands of Guatemala with a much more evolved culture (including the customs of building temples, carving stone, and writing) who acted as a major catalyst. At any rate, population must have reached a level sufficient to attract foreigners, and an integral swidden system was probably already in vogue in some areas. By A.D. 900 this huge region was densely settled, the scene of perhaps the greatest experiment in swidden agriculture in human history.

Although large nucleated settlements may occur with integral swidden agriculture, they do so only under conditions of extreme pressure, such as intensive warfare or the administrative needs of a state. Normally, population is distributed in small nucleated settlements or hamlets, or else is completely dispersed into neighborhoods. The former was the normal settlement pattern of the Classic Maya.

Settlement pattern studies reveal a stratification of territorial groups. The smallest level was the house group, a cluster of one to four pole-and-thatch dwellings built on separate stone-faced platforms and arranged around patios, presumably serving as residences of extended families. Between five and ten house groups composed a hamlet. By analogy with the historic Maya, the hamlet was probably inhabited by a localized patrilineage. An average of ten hamlets served, and were served by, a minor ceremonial center consisting of the two basic types of Maya buildings: temples on high terraced platforms, and multi-room buildings (referred to as *palaces*) on low platforms. The palaces probably functioned as residences for priests. Above this level were major ceremonial centers that included a series of plaza complexes frequently connected by paved roads and composed of scores of temples, palaces, altars, shrines, sweat baths, and ball courts. Most Maya painting, sculpture, and stucco-modeling consisted of ornamentation of buildings in major ceremonial centers; and all inscriptions are found in these centers. In no case is there evidence of urban concentration of population, in the Central Mexican sense, at these centers. This basic pattern of settlement seems to have been maintained throughout Classic Maya history, and it is doubtful whether any Maya polity (center and satellite settlements) had a population exceeding 20,000 inhabitants during Early Classic times.

Archaeologists and ethnologists, when considering the absence of cities, have been puzzled about the means by which Maya society was integrated.

---

[5] Harold C. Conklin, *Hunanoo Agriculture*, Food and Agricultural Organization of the United Nations, FAO Forestry Development Paper No. 12 (1957).

Vogt has, on the basis of parallelisms with the contemporary Maya of Zinacantan,[6] suggested that the ancient Maya may have had a part-time religious hierarchy in which the residents of hamlets rotated religious offices for specific periods, during which they resided at the ceremonial center and administered to the needs of the gods; upon completion of their tour of duty, they retired to the hamlet until ready to assume comparable or higher positions. By this means, nearly all adult males would participate in the religious cult, and Maya society would be integrated through the religious system. Possibly a few men of special ability would be selected for service as full-time priests. The strong focus in Maya art on religion and the lack of evidence of large residential populations at the centers are thus explained. Maya society (combined with patrisibs, on analogy with the historic Maya) may well have been structured in this manner in Formative and Protoclassic times. If evidence of foreign intrusion during the latter phase is correct, however, the immigrants probably dominated the full-time positions. In Early Classic times we see an increasing tendency toward the establishment of a large professional priesthood. The quality of Maya art would also argue for a class of professional artisans in full-time residence at the major centers. In all probability, the lay-priestly hierarchy continued to function and was used by the professional priesthood (as it was by the Catholic Church in the post-Conquest period) as a tool in achieving social integration.

By the end of the Early Classic phase (A.D. 300–600) Maya civilization had reached its maximal geographic extension, and all of the major ceremonial centers were functioning; the final century of the phase saw a sudden influx of influence from Teotihuacán. Along with the evidence noted previously, a remarkable event occurred that points towards a profound penetration by Teotihuacán into the social and religious life of the Maya elite: for a period of from 40 to 60 years there was, not only at Tikal but in all Maya centers, a cessation of the custom of erecting stelae with carved dates.

Following the collapse of Teotihuacán, the basic pattern of Maya life continued, and Late Classic (A.D. 600–900) witnessed the climactic development of Maya art and the maximal growth of population. It was also a phase of regional differentiation, now on the elite level. The art reflects a growing significance of competition, conflict and warfare, the establishment of larger political systems coordinated at huge macroceremonial centers, and the development of more aristocratic societal patterns with secular dynasties of Central Mexican type. It is possible that many elements of this new political system were derived from Teotihuacán and that ruling lineages may even have claimed descent from Central Mexicans as did Postclassic Maya from their Toltec conquerors. Tikal grew into an enormous center with hundreds of public buildings and elite residences. Urbanism did not evolve, however, and Maya centers remained essentially ceremonial and administrative. Even the macrocenters controlled relatively small districts when compared with the domain of Classic and Postclassic empires of the Central Plateau. The Maya sociopolitical system was not expansive in the Central Mexican sense.

[6] Evon Z. Vogt, "Some Aspects of Zinacantan Settlement Patterns and Ceremonial Organization," *Estudios de Cultural Maya*, vol. 1 (Mexico: Universidad Nacional Autónoma de Mexico), pp. 131–146.

When Spaniards arrived in the 16th century, they found the Maya still in possession of the northern third of Yucatan and a narrow strip along the east and west coasts (the alluvial plain of Tabasco and western Honduras)—in other words, the peripheries of Classic Maya territory. A huge region in the center of the peninsula, the Classic demographic heartland, was virtually uninhabited. The magnitude and nature of the Maya decline is clearly not the product of any single factor; but some kind of ecological disaster was involved. The most convincing argument is that intensive practice of swidden for one thousand years gradually resulted in deterioration of soil and conversion of much of the region into artificial savanna. Although Neolithic cultivators could theoretically cope with this problem, declining yields and increasing labor of cultivation, combined with the growing demands of an expanding class of nonfood producers, must have caused considerable peasant unrest and dissatisfaction; intensification of warfare in Late Classic times and evidence of nutritional deficiencies are reflections of these problems. The result may have been widespread revolt, followed by emigration to the frontiers once the controls exercised by the ruling class vanished.

The Toltec Empire

Following the collapse of Teotihuacán in the Central Plateau, three major highland centers shared in the spoils: Cholula, Xochicalco, and Tula. All were located within the core territory of the Early Classic state, but only Cholula was an important provincial center during the apogee of Teotihuacán. Archaeological evidence strongly indicates that Teotihuacán collapsed under pressure of internal troubles and that Cholula was probably the leader of the revolt.

The Late Classic phase in Central Mexico was essentially a period of struggle for power between the three centers. Cholula grew into an enormous city (covering an area of at least 8 sq. km), and during this phase was constructed the largest building ever erected by American Indians—a temple platform 60 m high with a base covering 10 ha. Cholula was the center of development for a distinctive epigraphic system and a new synthesis of Central Mexican religion (see below) that diffused widely over Mesoamerica during the Postclassic. It was also the probable source of a distinctive polychrome ceramic complex (the Mixteca–Puebla) that was widely traded and imitated. Cholula's tributary domain apparently included most of the present state of Puebla with adjacent portions of Oaxaca and Vera Cruz.

Xochicalco in Morelos is a large site sprawling over two high hills, a number of smaller ones, and an adjacent plateau. One of the hills was elaborately terraced and covered with public buildings (temples, palaces, ball courts, shrines) and elite and lower-class residences; it was defended by a system of moats and breastworks. The total area of the center was between 200 and 300 ha. The domain of the city was apparently limited to the present state of Morelos.

Aztec annals speak of an earlier people, the Toltecs, who were accomplished architects and artists and who ruled a great empire from a city called Tollan. According to the history, they were a "chosen" people, led by a magician-priest, who immigrated to Central Mexico from the north. A careful examination of place-names mentioned in Toltec history places the capital on a low ridge overlooking a contemporary town that still bears the name Tula or Tollan. Although we are generally skeptical of the historical veracity of migration legends (almost all groups have them, and the Toltec type has obvious political overtones), there is convincing archaeological evidence for this one. During the Late Classic there was a small town at one end of the ridge. We know little about the architecture, since the site has not been excavated; however, the ceramics (referred to as *Coyotlatelco*) show unmistakable derivation from Teotihuacán. The town was apparently founded by a rebel group that had participated in the destruction of the Early Classic city. At approximately the point where most archaeologists end the Classic period there are indications of a major social upheaval in the history of the town. The Late Classic location was abandoned and a new town founded on the opposite end of the ridge. This event was accompanied by major changes in ceramics—the Mazapan phase. The new pottery has strong stylistic links to pottery from the Bajío (situated to the north). In all probability there was a genuine migration, perhaps of a warrior band who usurped control over the Late Classic state, and the annals may refer to this event.

During the Late Formative the northwestern frontier of Mesoamerica was occupied by sedentary farmers, and population reached a level sufficient to permit military adventuring of the type noted by the end of the Classic. The epic struggle between the natives and the invaders was immortalized in later Aztec myths as a struggle between two religions, one led by the priest-king Quetzalcoatl and the other by the warrior-chief Tezcatlipoca, both of whom became gods in the Aztec pantheon. Tezcatlipoca was victorious and Quetzalcoatl driven out; however, the conflict apparently led to only a partial victory for the foreigners, since the resultant elite culture of Tula is essentially derived from Teotihuacán.

In the struggle for power between Tula, Xochicalco, and Cholula, it was the Toltecs at Tula who emerged as victors. Xochicalco was abandoned and Cholula relegated to a local religious and commercial center. It was at Tula also that the older Teotihuacán tradition and religious concepts from Cholula and the northern barbarians were syncretized into a distinctive new Great Tradition that archaeologists call Postclassic. The core concept was that the earth was destined for destruction unless the sun could be sustained, that the sun could be sustained only by human blood and hearts, and that certain aristocratic lineages were selected by the gods to achieve this end. The Toltecs were the first people chosen for this task, and their victims were obtained through warfare.

Toltec art emphasized ritualism in warfare—it is replete with such motifs as warriors, symbols of warrior societies (felines, eagles, canines), skulls, human hearts, and long bones. It would be a serious mistake, however, to assume that the primary motivation for Toltec warfare was ritualistic; the underlying functions were clearly economic. What is involved is a validation of political power and its military base. The older Teotihuacán gods—Tláloc, Huehueteotl, and Xipe—survived, but with altered functions and characteristics, and to them were added Tezatlipoca and Quetzalcoatl.

The tributary domain of Tula apparently extended over the Central Plateau and a large area of the northwest frontier. Toltec influence in religious art and architecture, however, was widespread over southern Mesoamerica. According to tradition, one band of Toltec adventurers led by the banished Quetzalcoatl conquered the Maya of northern Yucatan and built an enormous center at Chichen Itzá that duplicates, detail for detail, the architecture and sculpture of Tula. Temples closely imitating the Toltec style are found as far afield as highland Guatemala. During the period of Toltec political and cultural domination, trade was intense and widespread, and it was at this time that metallurgy was introduced, apparently from the south. According to tradition, Tula was destroyed and Toltec power broken by barbarian invasions in the 12th century. The tremendous impact of Tula continued to be felt, however; the content of the Late Postclassic represents essentially a continuation of Toltec culture. Many of the petty dynasts of the later phase claimed descent from the royal lineage of Tula. One of these dynasties was the Aztec, who were ultimately to succeed the Toltecs as rulers of Mesoamerica.

The Aztec Empire

Following the collapse of Tula, Central Mexico dissolved into a great number of competing states. Some of the ruling lineages claimed descent from the Toltec dynasty, others from the barbarian invaders from the north. Among the latter were the Aztec. The Late Postclassic phase was one of increasing aridity in the northwestern Mesoamerican frontier. This process undoubtedly had repercussions on the chiefdoms located on the margins, or within the frontiers, of the Toltec state; Tula's demise was probably the product of invasions and population movements southward. However, evidence from Aztec ceramics points strongly towards a local origin for Aztec culture, and strong continuities on the elite level of Toltec and Aztec culture argue against massive population displacements.

At any rate, the official version of early Aztec history repeats early Toltec history: a chosen people, led by a magician-priest (Huitzilopochtli, who is later deified as the God of War), assume the role of sustainers of the gods. What we are dealing with here is obviously a style of writing history rather than with history itself; in other words, a mythological validation of power. The Aztec founded their capital of Tenochtitlán in 1325 and obtained a member of the Toltec-derived dynastic line of neighboring Cúlhuacan as king in 1376. After an initial phase of military misfortunes, the Aztec formed an alliance with the two neighboring states of Texcoco and Tlacopan in 1427. Under the reigns of six successive rulers, terminating with the ill-fated Moctezuma, their warriors conquered a huge territory that embraced 200,000 sq. km and a population of 5,000,000–6,000,000—the largest polity in Mesoamerican history.

Archaeological and documentary literature on the Aztec is enormous and here we can only touch upon some of the major features of this complex civilization. The capital of Tenochtitlán was a huge center, comparable in size and population to Teotihuacán, located on two islands and on artificially-produced land within Lake Texcoco. The city was connected to the mainland and to a constellation of smaller cities and towns by three great masonry causeways, each several kilometers in length. Water was brought in by a masonry aqueduct. Tenochtitlán was originally two cities that united politically while continuing to maintain two civic centers, one in Tenochtitlán proper, the other in Tlateloco. The Tenochtitlán center included a sacred enclosure that measured 400 m to a side, within which were temples, priestly dormitories, colleges, a ball court, and a variety of shrines. Adjoining the enclosure were the royal palaces of a succession of kings—that of Moctezuma is reported as having had 300 rooms—and a variety of other public buildings. The causeways met at this center and served as major traffic arteries. The exact plan of the city as a whole is not known, but it apparently consisted of a regular grid of streets and canals. The Tlatelolco civic center consisted of a huge market and a second large religious precinct. The city was divided into five great wards (including Tlatelolco as one), each of which was sub-divided into 12–15 smaller wards, and these in turn had civic-ceremonial precincts. The total amount of public construction at Tenochtitlán must have rivaled Teotihuacán; Spanish accounts are unequivocal as to the urban status of the Aztec capital. Smaller wards were occupied by endogamous craft guilds, and specialization involved almost all Aztec technology. Spanish statements indicate that much of the specialization was full-time, but many craftsmen were also farmers, cultivating lands on the mainland or *chinampas*.

Chinampas are artificial islands constructed of layers of mud and vegetation within shallow fresh water lakes. This technique of land reclamation was initiated in Toltec times but reached its maximal development in the 16th century. Almost all of Lake Xochimilco was converted to chinampas by 1519. The Aztec even converted a large bay of saline Lake Texcoco into a freshwater lake by a system of sluiced dikes and spring-fed aqueducts, and covered it with chinampas. The rich organic soil and readily available moisture, combined with techniques of fertilization and the use of seed beds, converted the lakes into a major agricultural resource. Chinampa cultivation represents the final stage of ecological adaptation of the Mesoamerican farmer to the Basin of Mexico. By 1519, the combination of chinampa agriculture, canal and floodwater irrigation, and terracing supported the densest population in the history of the culture area.

From this geopolitical heartland the Aztec ruled their vast tributary domain. The hundreds of small conquered states were organized into 38 tributary provinces, each with a provincial capital, an Aztec governor, a garrison, and a cadre of tax-collectors. The Aztec did not reorganize subject states—they simply collected tribute from local rulers. The major function of the governor was to supervise tax collection, although some documentary evidence indicates that he had judicial functions as well and that the Aztec were attempting to establish a single legal code. They were also in the process of converting the Nahua speakers of the Basin of Mexico into a kind of core nationality of the empire. Garrisons were supplied with soldiers from a great number of formerly independent small states in this area, and all ruling lineages were interrelated by marriage. The Spaniards even report a syndicate of professional merchants (the Pochteca), membership of which cross-cut local states and was centered at the capital. These points deserve emphasis because most anthropologists have overstated the case in describing the Aztec political system as simply a city-state forcibly exacting tribute from other states.

The nerve center of this political machine was the ruler's palace in Tenochtitlán, and again there are a number of misconceptions in the literature. Moctezuma was a king in every sense of the word. Service's description of the Ancient State precisely describes the Aztec political system. The Aztec state was characterized by two features common to all states: departmentalization and a chain of command. Departments included war, finance, judiciary, religion, and the executive; each was internally complex. The judiciary, for example, included a pyramid of courts, each with judges, scribes, and a police force; the finance department included a small army of tax-receivers, scribes, royal craftsmen, and laborers.

Aztec society was divided into three well-defined endogamous castes. On top were *Pilli*, nobles by birth, including all descendants of previous and reigning rulers by legimate wives. Below was the largest caste, the *Macehual*, subdivided into a number of status levels or classes with professional warriors (an achieved status) at the top, merchants and elite craftsmen below them, and craftsmen and farmers following in succession. At the bottom of the scale was a depressed caste, the *Mayeques*, serfs attached to the estates of nobles or to estates assigned to political offices. These levels were differentiated in the tax-collecting system; for example, all were required to pay military service to the ruler, but Pillis and warriors were exempt from all other taxes, whereas craftsmen and merchants paid additional taxes with goods of their trade. Heaviest obligations fell on the farmers, who not only were taxed in agricultural produce but were also subject to corvee labor drafts. Administrative positions were filled primarily from the Pilli and warrior levels.

In summary, the Aztec political and economic system represents the end of a long tradition of societal evolution that began with the first attempts at plant domestication in the arid uplands of Mesoamerica and reached its climactic development in the same region.

Six   Tribe to Empire
in the Central Andes

The Central Andes as a culture area included the highlands of Peru and Bolivia and the coastal plain of Peru.[1] As in Mesoamerica, its history is one of regional stylistic diversity within an overall pattern of basic uniformity; Central Andean society went through a series of stages of societal development from tribe to empire. The specific profile of Central Andean history shows some remarkable parallelisms to Mesoamerican history, similarities that have stimulated diffusionist arguments; but there are striking differences that weaken the forces of these same arguments. Of particular interest are differences in precocity in appearance of societal and technological stages in the two areas. Regional differences within the Central Andes can be seen, particularly those between the highlands and coastal desert regions, and Andean archaeologists have long noted stylistic variations between northern, central, and southern segments of each of the two regions. Ecological differ-

---

[1] The following works provide a useful general introduction to the contents of this chapter: Wendell C. Bennett and Junius B. Bird, *Andean Culture History*, Handbook Series, no. 15 (New York: Museum of Natural History, 1949); Geoffrey H. S. Bushnell, *Peru* (New York: Frederick A. Praeger, Inc., 1963); Edward P. Lanning, *Peru before the Incas* (Englewood Cliffs, N.J.: Prentice-Hall, Inc., 1967); and J. Alden Mason, *The Ancient Civilizations of Peru* (Magnolia, Mass.: Peter Smith, Publisher, 1957).

ences between highlands and lowlands, however, are not of the same order as those between highlands and tropical lowlands of Mesoamerica, and consequently the intensity of regional differentiation in the Central Andes is much less. During periods of stylistic unity, Central Andean history differs from similar periods in Mesoamerica in that its unity of culture is greater; Andean horizon styles are more pervasive and influence local art styles more profoundly. This undoubtedly reflects differences in level of political integration, and the frequently noted differences between Aztec and Inca in this respect are illustrated in the archaeology.

In the chapter on Mesoamerica we began with a brief summary of characteristics of the area as a whole, based on comparison of various regional groups, and at the end of the chapter we discussed characteristics of the Aztec state. Owing to the striking uniformity of culture of the Central Andes at Contact (the product of Inca acculturation), we can eliminate this introductory summary and will delay discussion of the Contact culture until the end.

From Tribe to Chiefdom

In Mesoamerica ceramics and sedentary village life appear at about the same time. In the Central Andes sedentary village life, based on a combination of cultivation and intensive utilization of marine resources, predates pottery and began as early as 3600 B.C. on the Central and South Coasts, as we have seen. Tribal societies were definitely established between 3600 and 2500 B.C. in the pre-Cotton phase; in the succeeding post-Cotton phase they appear on the North Coast as well. During this latter phase, indications of a complex society emerged in a series of adjacent coastal valleys from Nepeña to Chillón. At a short distance from the sea the Casma Valley drops from an alluvial terrace to a narrow coastal plain. On the plain is a large site, called Las Haldas, of stone houses and public buildings. The site has two major occupations, a pre-Ceramic and an Early Formative. The earlier occupation was the heavier, and occupational remains of this period cover 200 ha.[2] Associated with the earlier phase are massive ceremonial buildings. The largest is a compound 450 m long within which were seven stone-faced temple platforms. The complex was rebuilt a number of times, and its earliest construction levels are of the pre-Ceramic phase. Two C14 dates of 1640 and 1842 B.C. are reported for this occupation level. Lanning reports a site of comparable size, with a similar civic center, at Chuquitanta in the Chillón Valley; the associated C14 date is 1850 B.C.[3] Well-developed chiefdoms probably appear in this section of the coast, shortly after or before 2000 B.C., at least six centuries before their appearance in Mesoamerica. Elsewhere along the coast, populations remained small, with society on a tribal level. In some South Coast valleys many settlements were tightly

[2] John H. Rowe, "Urban Settlements in Ancient Peru," *Nawpa Pacha*, I (1963), pp. 1–37.
[3] Edward P. Lanning, "Early Man in Peru," *Scientific American*, CCXIII, 4 (1965), pp. 68–76.

nucleated and had relatively large populations, up to a few thousand inhabitants. Rowe has labeled these settlements *urban*, but he is clearly referring to the simple fact of nucleation and not to the type of internal societal differentiation that we mean by the term. The sites are comparable in many ways to the villages of the historic Anasazi in the American Southwest.

Results of recent excavations at Kotosh, near Húanuco, indicate that the North Highlands had reached comparable development at about the same time. Japanese archaeologists have excavated a large temple that was the product of twelve successive building-phases; they have also associated six ceramic phases with the buildings, all Formative in date, the earliest beginning around 1800 B.C. Of particular significance is the fact that the earliest building, with modeled clay ornamentation (a life-size human figure with crossed hands), predates the earliest ceramics.

The history of the Central Andes, following the inception of pottery-making, has been organized in a variety of ways. The following scheme will be used in this study: The term Formative refers to the period between 1800 B.C. and A.D. 1, which may be subdivided into four phases: Initial (1800–1200 B.C.), a phase when ceramics were limited to the Northern Highlands; Early (1200–750 B.C.), characterized by a rapid diffusion of monochrome ceramics over most of the Central Andes; Middle (750–400 B.C.), a phase during which the highly evolved Chavin art style diffused over most of the coastal plain and the Northern Highlands; and Late (400 B.C.–A.D. 1), a phase during which numerous regional styles emerged that provided the base for evolution of the great Classic styles. The Formative Period is followed by Classic (A.D. 1–800) and Postclassic (A.D. 800–1530).

For societal evolution, our best data for the Initial and Early Ceramic comes from the Pacific Coast, where, during the Initial phase in the highlands, pottery was still absent. The culture of that phase was essentially a continuation of the post-Cotton, pre-Ceramic phase previously described. Chiefdoms were present in the valleys from Nepeña to Chillón, and tribal societies were in the valleys to the north and south. This pattern continues through the Early Formative except in the Casma Valley, where we have evidence of respectable population in inland locations and the beginnings of primary dependence on agriculture.[4] Las Haldas, however, remains the chiefdom center. By the end of Early Formative times, the Central Andes from Ecuador to Bolivia—both coast and highland—was occupied by pottery-making village farmers.

With these events the stage was set for the emergence of the first truly elaborate culture and sophisticated religious art in the history of the culture area. This culture and style is referred to as *Chavín*, dates from the Middle Formative, and is the Andean counterpart—historically and with respect to societal evolution—of the Olmec in Mesoamerica.

The site of Chavín is in the Mosna Valley, a tributary of the Marañón, in the Northern Highlands, nearly 3200 m above sea level. It consists of two components: a civic center and an attached residential area. The civic center

---

[4] Donald E. Thompson, "Formative Period Architecture in the Casma Valley, Peru," *Actas y Memorias del XXV Congreso Internacional de Americanistas* (Mexico, 1964), pp. 205–212.

is located on a triangular plain delimited by the Mosna, a permanent stream, and by a tributary barranca. The entire area (6 ha) was artificially landscaped by retaining walls and terraces.

The major architectural complex consists of a sunken court paved with stone, 48 m square, delimited by low platforms on the north and south and by the Castillo, a massive terraced platform, on the west. The Castillo is constructed of earth and rock, has a dressed stone retaining wall, stands 13 m high, and has a basal dimension 75 m square. Superficially it resembles a Mesoamerican temple platform since it is accompanied by ascending stairways and summit buildings. The buildings, however, are very small, and the major activities seem to have taken place within, rather than on, the summit of the platform. The interior is honeycombed with long galleries that provided access to a series of small niche-like rooms. The gallery-room complexes are arranged on several levels connected by ramps or stairways and provided with elaborate ventilation systems.

A series of life-size stone heads of humans with deeply wrinkled faces and felinized humans (or anthropomorphic felines) were tenoned in the retaining wall. Along the upper edge of the wall was a projecting cornice with carved designs in a relief technique so shallow it could be described as incision. The same type of carving was applied to round columns at the building's portal and to stelae; one of which latter, the Lanzón, was found within a niche-room. The Castillo clearly had a religious function, but its specific use is not clear. It resembles a funerary monument: the great number of galleries (there is evidence that the other platforms were similarly structured of galleries and rooms), the lack of provision for light, and the limited access (by a few small entrances set into the retaining wall), all point in this direction, but direct evidence of burials has not been reported.

Most Chavín carvings have as their central theme a feline or felinized human, but others focus on fish, raptorial birds, or a composite crocodilian monster. The style emphasizes curved lines, is extraordinarily intricate, with great numbers of small figures (usually cats) disposed within and around the body and clothing of the central figures. Characteristic of the feline representation is a U-shaped mouth and crossed fangs. Associated with the sculpture and architecture is a monochrome ceramic complex that emphasizes tecomates, flat-bottomed bowls and collared jars, and contrasting zones of roughened and polished surfaces, incision, and punctation.

Chavín has been described as a ceremonial center inhabited by a few professional priests and artisans and supported by periodic and voluntary contributions from a rural population dispersed over a large surrounding territory. On the other hand, recent surveys by Rowe[5] have revealed a nucleated settlement, covering at least 50 ha, that underlies the modern village adjacent to the civic center. The specific combination of architecture, sculpture, and ceramics found at Chavín furthermore is limited to a relatively small region. Surveys by Tello[6] report a large number of small, contemporary villages and civic centers in the Mosna Valley. The data therefore indicate

[5] Rowe, *op. cit.*, 1–27.

[6] Julio C. Tello, *Arqueología del Valle de Casma, Culturas: Chavín, Santo o Huaylas Yunga y Sub-Chimu*, and *Chavín, Cultural Matriz de la Civilizacion Andina, Primera Parte*, Publication Antropologica del Archivo "Julio C. Tello," vols. I, II (Lima: Universidad Nacional Mayor de San Marcos, 1956).

that Chavín was a relatively large, nucleated center of a small, compact, densely settled polity—most probably a chiefdom.

The central religious symbol of Chavín, the anthropomorphic feline, is widely distributed over the North Highlands and the North and Central Coast. It is found on pottery, textiles, in beaten gold, in wood, and stone. Found throughout the Central Andes in Middle Formative times is a monochrome ceramic tradition emphasizing tecomate and flat-bottomed bowl forms and plastic design. Some writers have referred to this ceramic complex as Chavín or Chavinoid and have assigned the style a much wider distribution. This broadening of definition, however, weakens the historical significance of the style, since in all probability several of the ceramic traits did not originate in areas of the Chavín religious style.

Even within the orbit of Chavín style there is considerable variation. On the coast, for example, two pottery forms—the long-necked bottle and stirrup-spouted jar (both to have long subsequent histories)—are characteristic; both are rare at Chavín, while rocker-stamping as a technique of decorating pottery is much more common at Ancón and Supe than elsewhere. More importantly, there is a considerable range in societal evolution: in the Virú Valley (on the North Coast) society remained on a tribal level; in Cupisnique Quebrada, further up the coast, Larco Hoyle has described a more complex Middle Formative society.[7] Although monumental architecture has not been reported, there are cemeteries of deep shaft tombs containing elaborate funerary offering, pottery, and personal ornaments of lapis lazuli, bone, shell, stone, and quartz. Pottery is often elaborately modeled or incised, not only with Chavín symbols, but with representations of a variety of plants and animals. Also modeled is a dual personage represented with a split face. None of these is specifically a Chavín symbol.

Local cultures elsewhere are generally comparable in level to either Virú or Cupisnique, with one notable exception: in two neighboring North Coast Valleys, Casma and Nepeña (note that they were also precocious in the pre-Ceramic period), the Middle Formative Culture rivaled that of Chavín. Following the Early Formative phase in Casma, the center of Las Haldas on the coastal plan was abandoned, and the Middle Formative phase witnessed a population explosion extending up valley and accompanied by large-scale irrigation, the earliest appearance of this new ecosystem in the Central Andes. Elsewhere along the coast, cultivation was of the floodwater type and subsistence remained tied to the littoral. There is evidence that these events were linked to the introduction of a more productive variety of maize. Also present in Casma were large civic centers. One, Sechín Alto, includes one of the largest buildings erected in Central Andean history (a mammoth platform 35 m high and 250 x 300 m in basal dimensions). Building types included terraced stone and earth platforms with stairways—and whole plaza complexes of temples on their summits (the Castillo type interior galleries are absent)—and smaller temples composed of courtyards and sanctuaries, enclosed by compounds and placed on low basal platforms.

One site, Moxexe, is of particular interest. The center had a terraced oval temple platform 30 m high and a series of huge conjoined rectangular en-

[7] Rafael Larco Hoyle, *Los Cupisniques* (Lima: Casa editora "La Cronica" y "Variedades" S.A., 1941).

closures delimited by massive low rock walls (probably the bases of high adobe walls); most of these are empty, but one encloses hundreds of conjoined rooms arranged along streets—possibly a warehouse or laborers' quarters. The site also includes great numbers of room complexes placed on adjoining low platforms and arranged around courts. Moxexe was clearly a large, nucleated, partially-planned center with public buildings of monumental size. Also associated with Casma Valley sites are life-size painted figures modeled in clay (and placed in niches within platform retaining walls) in Chavín style, and incised stone carvings in a style only remotely related to Chavín. The settlement pattern at Moxexe suggests a social structure closer to a state than a chiefdom, and the transition may well have taken place in the Casma Valley in Middle Formative times.

One of the major controversies of Central Andean archaeology has been concerned with the origin of Chavín religious concepts and art style, and the mechanism of their diffusion. The major debate is whether Chavín had a coastal or a highland origin. Recent data from Kotosh would favor a source in the North Highlands.[8] The Chavín-influenced ceramic phase at Kotosh begins around 1000 B.C., two centuries earlier than on the coast; it may be somewhat earlier in inception at Chavín itself. Evidence from Kotosh also indicates derivation of Chavín pottery from earlier ceramic complexes in the same general region. Some writers have argued a completely non-Andean origin, primarily a Mesoamerican one. Discussion of this will be reserved until the final chapter.

With respect to diffusion of the Chavín style, the explanation offered for diffusion of Olmec style in Mesoamerica applies here as well: it was clearly not the center of an empire; diffusion most likely occurred via trade contacts organized by North Highland chiefdoms. With respect to the Central Andes, the origin of chiefdoms as a whole, the origin of the state, and the origin and diffusion of the Chavín style are separate historical processes, and should not be considered a single historical problem.

In summary, the Early and Middle Formative witnessed two major developments. The first was the spread of the village level of the Central Andean cultural pattern over almost the entire culture area—nearly all historic Andean crops were cultivated by the end of the Middle Formative, the Andean domestic animals were present, and irrigation and terracing were initiated in a number of areas. The second development was the appearance of the elite level of historical Central Andean technology in some areas. Stone and earth public architecture, large residential sites, stone sculpture, the beginnings of metallurgy (though the utilitarian tool kit is still based on chipped and polished stone), heddle-loom weaving (with both tapestry and embroidery), sophisticated ceramics, specialized military equipment (clubs, slings, spear-throwers, and even forts) were all present in a number of areas.

The subsequent Late Formative is essentially characterized by wider distribution of the elite level of Andean culture. On the North Coast military architecture, large adobe temple platforms, irrigation, population expansion upvalley (a process similar to that which occurred in Casma in Middle Formative times), and large nucleated settlements all appear for the first

---

[8] Seiichi Izumi and Toshihiko Sono, *Andes 2, Excavations at Kotosh, Peru* (Tokyo: Kadokawa Publishing Co., 1963), Ch. 8.

time. A great elaboration of burial ritual characterizes the South Coast, with status cemeteries of deep-shaft chamber tombs containing great quantities of textiles and pottery vessels. Other features appearing in the South Coast sequence at this time are adobe temple complexes and large, fortified, nucleated settlements. In the southern highlands monumental stone sculpture and architecture appear at Pucará and Tiahuanaco associated with relatively large, nucleated, residential centers.

Particularly diagnostic of the phase is a striking development of regional styles—the relative unity produced by diffusion of Chavín religious ideology is dissipated. Two technological developments in pottery have widespread distribution, proving extensive contact and diffusion between groups; these are white and red bichrome painting and negative painting. The first apparently originated on the North Coast or the North Highlands and diffused southwards. Negative painting was earliest on the South Coast and diffused north. Both have been considered as horizon styles in the Chavín, Tiahuanaco, and Inca sense, but they clearly are not styles at all. Foreshadowing later events, Late Formative represents a phase in which the great regional Classic civilizations germinated.

Regional States:
The Classic Period

The Classic Period saw an intensification of the regionalism that emerged in Late Formative times. It was also a period of spectacular development of stone sculpture, ceramics, textiles, architecture, and true metallurgy. Some craft products were so highly developed aesthetically that many archaeologists consider the period a cultural climax for the Central Andes and see the succeeding Postclassic as a period of cultural regression. Again, there are striking parallels to archaeological reconstructions of the history of Mesoamerican art. Regional ceramic styles pertaining to this period are Nazca on the South Coast, Interlocking on the Central Coast, Mochica on the North Coast, Recuay in the Callejón de Huayllas, Cajamarca in far North Highlands, and Tiahuanaco on the Bolivian Plateau. The central highlands from Ayacucho to Cuzo were apparently still lightly settled and characterized by a simple village culture. The following discussion will relate primarily to the two most highly developed regional cultures of the period, the Mochica and Tiahuanaco civilizations.

One of the best known of all the pre-Inca cultures of the Central Andes is that of the North Coast Mochica (named after the historic population of the North Coast). This knowledge derives from a number of sources, from intensive survey and excavations, but more particularly from Mochica art with its extraordinary range of subject matter. Mochica funerary ceramics, consisting primarily of stirrup-spouted vessels (decorated by modeled and painted scenes), provide an almost complete ethnographic record. Subject matter includes gods and religious ceremonies, craft activities, architecture, disease, crime and punishment, court ritual, hunting, fishing, agriculture, warfare, tribute-collecting, and erotica, all done in an exquisitely realistic style.

Mochica funerary ceramic style went through five evolutive phases. It originated in the Moche and Chicama valleys and during its later phases expanded into all the coastal valleys between Jequetepeque and Casma, suddenly and abruptly eclipsing local styles. These events strongly suggest conquest and there is much corroborative evidence this was the case.

Mochica subsistence was based primarily on agriculture, with herding and fishing as secondary activities. All the historic Andean cultigens were known. Large pan-valley centralized irrigation systems were fully evolved, and population may have reached a peak for many coastal valleys during this period. Metallurgy was very highly developed and included such techniques as hammering repoussé, embossing, lost-wax and open-mold casting, soldering, welding, annealing, alloying, gilding, and inlay. Metals used were gold, silver, and copper. Metal was smelted from ores as well as secured in pure state and was used for ornaments, weapons, and even for agricultural tools. Pottery funerary vessels were produced in molds, as were a variety of other ceramic artifacts: stamps, spindle whorls, musical instruments (pan pipes, trumpets, flutes, whistles), and figurines. Only a little Mochica weaving has survived, and this indicates a high level of skill.

The best data available on Mochica settlement patterns are from Virú. Willey [9] has defined three basic settlement types for the Gallinazo phase, the local Classic culture that precedes Mochica conquest; they may be classified as small agglutinated villages, large agglutinated villages, and agglutinated towns. All three are characterized by complexes of conjoined rooms. The small sites have fewer than 100 rooms and are found in dry washes or hillsides along the edge of the narrow upper valley; the two larger types are found in the wider alluvial plain of the lower valley and contain up to several thousand rooms. The small villages could have been residences of single lineages, while the towns resemble large villages but include civic centers composed of courts delimited by large terraced temple platforms and smaller civic buildings. In one case, the Gallinazo Group, six large villages and towns are located within an area of only a few sq. km, forming a single great settlement that apparently served as a capital. These settlement types continued during the period of Mochica domination with a new type added, the provincial capital. This is essentially a smaller version of the capital of the Mochica state described below. Another site type in Virú during the Classic Period is represented by great fortresses consisting of terraced adobe platforms with room complexes and defensive peripheral walls, built on spurs or isolated hills overlooking the valley.

The Mochica capital was probably the site of Moche, located on the south edge of the Moche Valley. The site includes two huge buildings separated by an enormous plaza and surrounded by an extensive residential zone. One of the buildings, the Huaca de La Luna, is a massive, terraced, multi-room structure built against the flank of a hill; it probably served as the palace of the ruler. The second, Huaca del Sol, is a gigantic temple platform 18 m high with a basal platform measuring 228 × 136 m, constructed in five narrow, ledgelike terraces. On the summit of the south end is a second terraced platform 23 m high and 103 m square. Ramps provided access to

---

[9] Gordon R. Willey, *Prehistoric Settlement Patterns in the Virú Valley, Peru*, Bureau of American Ethnology Bulletin No. 155 (Washington: Smithsonian Institution, 1953).

temple complexes on the summit. Mochica construction was primarily of mold-made, rectangular adobe bricks. In some temples are mural paintings executed in a style directly comparable to the painting on pottery.

The quality of Mochica craftsmanship, particularly in elite crafts, and the use of mass production techniques, such as are implied by the mold in ceramics and metallurgy, indicate the work of full-time craftsmen. This is also demonstrated by scenes on Mochica pots that show craftsmen working under supervisors. Many other scenes, modeled and painted on pottery, portray a definite hierarchical factor in Mochica social life that is supported by evidence from burials and house types. Scenes show men carried on sedan chairs, seated on canopied thrones, receiving tribute, and presiding at executions of wrongdoers. Others show individuals with specialized functions indicated by their dress: rulers, nobles, priests, warriors, slaves, messengers, craftsmen, servants, fishermen, hunters, and farmers. Warfare is a common theme in Mochica art. The evidence from ceramics for a Mochica conquest of neighboring valleys was noted; this is strongly supported by the presence of provincial centers built in Mochica style and by transvalley roads. Corroborative evidence is also presented by pottery vessels in the form of skillfully modeled human heads that undoubtedly represent actual persons. They were reproduced in molds and placed in graves. Larco Hoyle [10] has demonstrated that some were kings (based on the fact that the same individual is found in all valleys) and that others represent provincial governors (their portraits are limited to a single valley); he has even shown that a number of different heads are representations of the same ruler or governor at different stages of his life.

In summary, archaeological data indicate that Mochica culture was the product of a highly centralized, aristocratically structured, aggressively militaristic, internally complex society—a society that can unhesitatingly be assigned to Service's Ancient State level of societal evolution.

Although proof is admittedly much less direct the Classic culture of Tiahuanaco, in the Bolivian Plateau, could be characterized in much the same way.

Tiahuanaco is one of the most impressive archaeological sites in the New World. It is located in treeless puna, 3842 m above sea level, approximately 21 km southeast of Lake Titicaca; it has suffered more destruction than perhaps any other major New World site, primarily because of post-Conquest looting for building-stone, and as a result it is much misunderstood. The site has been described as essentially a cluster of temples—each planned as a unit, but without overall planning of the center as a whole—and as lacking in associated habitation areas. Recent excavation by the Bolivian government and surveys by Rowe [11] have completely altered our understanding of the site. Rowe has defined a zone of continuous occupation covering an area of approximately 200 ha and stated that this is a minimal area for the urban zone since occupational debris extends considerably beyond it. Within the 200 ha zone is a central core 50 ha in extent which includes the public buildings that have made the site famous. Ibarra Grasso feels this core

[10] Raphael Larco Hoyle, *Los Mochicas* (Lima: Rimas, S.A., 1938–39), 2 vols.
[11] Rowe, *op. cit.*, 1–27.

exhibits overall planning and compares it to Teotihuacán.[12] He has defined two wide avenues, an east-west and a north-south that meet at a T-shaped intersection. The excavated structures in the core are oriented to these axes and may be classified according to four basic types: temples constructed on high, terraced platforms, temples built on low platforms, elite residences, and tombs.

The largest structure at Tiahuanaco is the Akapana. It has been described as a natural hill, regularized by retaining walls, that functioned as a refuge fort. Recent excavations indicate that it is an artificially terraced temple platform with a summit temple. It measures 140×180 m in basal dimension and is 15 m high. The Kalasasaya is an example of the second type of temple. It consists of a low platform 3 m high, with a basal dimension of 126×118 m. On the summit were small buildings that served as shrines and a sunken court inset into the body of the platform. The elite residences consist of rooms arranged around central courts. Other structures include small underground chambers that apparently served as tombs. Also found at the site is a system of underground water conduits.

Tiahuanaco architecture represents one of the climactic achievements of the American Indian. Special characteristics include use of large dressed stone blocks, perfectly fitted, and joined without mortar; temple doorways cut from a single block of stone; processional stairways in which each step is carved from a single block of stone; notched joining of stone blocks or joining by means of copper cramps; step-sided wall niches; and fitting of large blocks of stone into mosaic design. These techniques were applied to walls, roofs, and floors of temples and residences, attaining a climax in technique and artistry in the construction of the temple of Puma Puncu, where enormous blocks of stone, some weighing as much as 100 tons, were perfectly dressed, fitted, and joined.

Another striking feature of Tiahuanaco culture is stone sculpture: huge columnar statues, tenoned heads, and low-relief carving in a style that contrasts sharply with Chavín in its strongly rectilinear quality. Some relief carving resembles textile design.

Metallurgy was comparable in development to that on the North Coast. This is also thought to be true of the textile craft, though the evidence is largely indirect. Tiahuanaco ceramics contrast sharply with the emphasis on realistic modeling and narrative theme so characteristic of Mochica. The more elaborate ware is painted in white design outlined in black on a highly polished red slip; the design emphasizes religious symbols, cats, and humans painted in a lively, cartoonlike style. A distinctive form, and one of considerable historical significance, is a drinking goblet.

Painted on pottery and carved in relief as the central figure on a monolithic gateway (Gateway of the Sun) is an anthropomorphic being that was apparently the central god of Tiahuanaco. He is elaborately costumed and holds a staff in each hand (Bushnell suggests rather that he is holding a spear-thrower and a quiver of darts).[13] Distinctive features include winglike projections from the eyes and a fan-shaped headdress ornamented with puma

---

[12] Dick E. Ibarra Grasso, *Prehistoria de Bolivia* (La Paz–Cochabamba: Editorial "Los Amigos del Libro," 1965).
[13] Bushnell, *op. cit.*, pp. 93–94.

heads. On each side of the central figure are 48 rectangular panels arranged in three rows. Each contains a human figure who is either running towards, or kneeling before, the central figure. The central figure has been identified as the prototype of the Inca creator-god Viracocha.

A curious statement, first made by Bennett [14] and repeated by a number of authors, is that Tiahuanaco could not have been a city, owing to the low productivity of the region—curious, indeed, considering that approximately half a million peasants now live in the Titicaca basin and are obviously able to support themselves. In fact, the huge lake, with its extensive alluvial plains on the west, north, and south sides, together with the surrounding hilly ranges, offers a well-balanced ecological setting for a dense population. The lake has substantial fishing resources and could also have served as a transportation artery. The lakeshore plain provides abundant agricultural land for the Andean high altitude grain-and-root crop complex, and, along with the neighboring hills, offers excellent pasture for llamas and alpacas. Finally, recent data presented by Parsons and Denevan [15] indicate that approximately 800 sq km of lakeside marsh was converted into a ditch and ridge system comparable in many of its features to chinampas in the Basin of Mexico. There is also proof of stone terracing on the nearby slopes dating from this period. In short, we disagree completely with previous analyses of the Bolivian Plateau, which characterized it as a habitat unfit for an advanced civilization. The region was comparable in many ways to the Basin of Mexico and Tiahuanaco was the first large urban center to evolve in Central Andean history.

The Classic Period in the Central Andes was a period of considerable stylistic diversity. It was also apparently a period of striking variations in societal level. To a much less degree this was also true of Classic Mesoamerica, where both chiefdoms and tribes managed to survive in marginal locations even within the social setting of the Teotihuacán Empire. In the Central Andes this variability in societal level seems more pronounced. There is a strong possibility that chiefdoms continued to function as the major societal type in the North Highlands and South Coast in Classic times. Nazca culture, for example, with its extraordinary development of polychrome ceramics and fine weaving, is characterized by a heavy emphasis on burial ritual and lack of emphasis on temple construction—except toward the end of its history, when the site of Cahuachi apparently was the center of a small multivalley state. In the Central Highlands the scanty archaeology we have would seem to suggest an almost tribal level with simple village crafts and an absence of architectural centers. The Classic in the Central Andes also contrasts with the Classic of Mesoamerica in the lack of truly large states and urban centers.

The Wari Empire
and Its Aftermath

The Postclassic Period in the Central Andes (A.D. 800–1532 A.D.) has been characterized as a period that saw maximal development of urbanism,

[14] Wendell C. Bennett, *Excavations at Tiahuanaco*, Anthropological Papers, XXXIV (New York: American Museum of Natural History, 1934).

[15] James J. Parsons and William M. Denevan, "Pre-Columbian Ridged Fields," *Scientific American* (July 1967), pp. 93–100.

the intensification of social stratification, and the initiation of urban planning and large empires. It is also characterized as a period in which monumental architecture shifted from religious to secular interests, and a period of general decline in aesthetic quality of crafts. All these generalizations are correct, but when so stated tend to obscure the fact that the Postclassic was essentially the final phase in the evolution of processes that had begun as far back as the Middle Formative. The apparent aesthetic decline was functionally related to other processes, *e.g.* increasing craft specialization involving emphasis on mass production, and replacement of religious and related ancestor cults as major integrating institutions by more purely political ones. Furthermore, the assessment is not quite accurate since metallurgy and architecture reached their peak of evolution during the Postclassic.

The Early Postclassic, referred to by most Andean specialists as the Expansionist Period, dates from A.D. 800 to 1250. It is characterized above all by geographic expansion of the Tiahuanaco art style and particularly by the religious symbolism it expresses. This brings us to the fascinating problem of the factors, processes, and sources of this expansion. To put the matter briefly, Tiahuanaco religious symbols (particularly the Feline God and Viracocha) are found in pottery and textiles over most of the Central Andes. Also diffused were specific vessel forms, particularly the drinking goblet and the black-and-white on red color combination.

Notably strong manifestations of the style are found on the South Coast, where it fused with, and ultimately dominated, the Classic Nazca style; on the Central Coast, where it replaced the Interlocking style; and on the North Coast, where it eclipsed dramatically and completely the vigorous Mochica artistic tradition. It is also found in an attenuated and strongly altered form in the North Highlands. It is, therefore, a genuine horizon style. This diffusion differs from that of the Chavín style in that diffusion of the Tiahuanaco art style replaced local styles that were as highly evolved.

No one doubts the ultimate origin of the style from Tiahuanaco; controversy has primarily involved the process of its diffusion. Recent evidence supports the belief—buttressed by the consensus of archaeological opinion— that spread of the style was the product of conquest and that much of the Central Andes was politically unified into a great empire comparable to that of the Inca. Tiahuanaco itself has been rejected as the capital for two reasons: first, it was argued Tiahuanaco was a nonaggressive, nonmilitaristic, theocratic society, and that the plateau region was too remote and thinly settled to have allowed of such a polity. This argument is no longer valid. A more defensible position has been based on the internal chronology of Tiahuanaco. By the time of expansion of the style, the local Tiahuanaco ceramic tradition had changed radically into a geometric style referred to as Decadent Tiahuanaco. It differs strikingly from coastal Tiahuanaco pottery, with the emphasis of the latter on religious symbols in design. Most archaeologists favored a point of diffusion of the style from a site either in the Central Highlands or on the Pacific Coast. It was thought that Tiahuanaco priests had introduced a religious system to this postulated center and that it was from there that the style diffused, in this case by conquest.

The site of Wari, located in the Central Highlands near Ayacucho, is the strongest candidate for capital of the empire. During the Classic Period the Ayacucho Valley had a small population dispersed into a great number of villages. In the 8th century the area came under heavy influence from Nazca, presumably as a result of its inclusion in a trade network engineered by the little Nazca state of Cahuachi. A rapid population growth followed, as well as a process of nucleation of the population into a number of rival towns. By approximately A.D. 800 the local sequence reveals sudden intrusion of Tiahuanaco religious motifs painted on large burial urns from high-status burials. Within a century, the entire population of the valley was nucleated at Wari; the site expanded to enormous size, becoming one of the largest residential sites in the New World (approximately 10 sq km). During the 9th century, a stylistic syncretism occurred in Wari ceramics of native, Nazca, and Tiahuanaco traditions. This new style diffused widely throughout the coast and Northern Highlands. Along with Tiahuanaco influences in the pottery, tenoned heads and statues in Tiahuanaco style occur at Wari as well. However, Tiahuanaco architectural styles did not diffuse, except for underground tombs.

Building at Wari consists primarily of thousands of multifamily residences, compounds with central courts, and narrow, corridorlike rooms. At least one temple has been defined; it is formed by a very large open enclosure, the walls of which were once covered with tenoned heads. The central core of the city was surrounded by a massive fortification wall. Construction contrasts sharply with Tiahuanaco: walls are built of mud and roughly split stone, surfaced with mud stucco and gypsum plaster, and apparently had flat masonry roofs. Many buildings were multistoried. The growth of Wari was apparently unplanned, and residential units are not ordered on a grid. Later in the history of the city, large areas of residences and open land were included in huge compounds or enclosures separated by narrow alleys. Although compounds or enclosures are old on the coast, and the idea may have been emulated by the Wari dynasts, it was more likely a reinvention. This conclusion is offered because continuities through time of the architectural form have not been demonstrated and because urban planning is more likely to evolve as a local process related to internal growth than as the product of simple diffusion.

The most convincing evidence that Wari was the center of an empire stems from settlement pattern data. On the North Coast unplanned communities of conjoined rooms continue, but are accompanied by planned communities placed within large compounds of the Wari type. They are probably administrative centers occupied by colonies of highlanders established to administer and control the conquered population, offering close parallels to the Inca system. Also present are large, empty enclosures like those at Wari. Even more striking evidence is provided by the construction of large, planned civic centers in pure Wari style that combine the functions of garrison-granary and temple at a number of places in the highlands (Pikillakta and Viracocha Pampa).

In the Southern Highlands recent archaeological evidence indicates that Tiahuanaco reached its maximal urban growth during the Early Postclassic and that it too was the center of a large state that included much of the Bolivian Highlands, Southern Highlands, and far south coast of Peru. Colonies were apparently established in northern Chile and northwestern Argentina as well. The two states and the regional styles that accompanied their expansion met at a buffer zone at the watershed between the Vilcanota and Titicaca Basins.

Both Wari and Tiahuanaco were apparently abandoned at about the same time. For perhaps a century or so after the fall of Wari, a certain level of unity persisted along the coast represented by what has been called the Tiahuanaco B horizon. The ceramics continue the tradition in some forms and in focus on a black-and-white on red polychrome painting, but surfaces were unpolished and design was much simpler—exclusively geometric and poorly executed. The sudden disappearance of Tiahuanaco religious symbolism coincident with the abandonment of the two great highland centers is further proof that the mechanism of diffusion of the style was political. In Bolivia, Tiahuanaco influence in ceramics persisted to the Inca conquest. The unity we see on the coast was possibly the product of a continuing large state centered at Pachacamac.

All over the Central Andes, following the collapse of Wari and Tiahuanaco, pan-Andean unity dissolved into a series of regional traditions. This was followed, a century before the Spanish Conquest, by a short phase of return to unity stimulated by the Inca empire. In the Central and South Highlands there was a general cultural regression: monumental architecture was limited to *chullpas*—or tombs—on the Bolivian Plateau, cities were abandoned, and the population was dispersed into a great number of small hamlets. Rowe suggests an analogy to the collapse of urban life in Europe following the fall of Rome.[16] On the coast, however, the Late Postclassic witnessed a climactic development of urban life and large political systems, in part the product of both Wari influence and the collapse of Wari; but the development can also be understood as the end of a long local process of evolutionary adaptation to the desert environment.

The largest coastal kingdom was that of the Chimu, who located their capital on the edge of the Moche Valley at Chan Chan, the largest urban center to develop in the Central Andean area. The Chimu state embraced a series of coastal valleys from Tumbéz in the north to Chancay on the south, a linear distance of 1000 km. Various authors have estimated the size of Chan Chan at between 15 and 30 sq km; the preserved remains cover 7 to 10 sq km. The most imposing architectural forms at Chan Chan are huge walled adobe compounds (some standing walls are 9 m high), the largest of which has an interior surface area of 17 ha. There are ten of these enormous structures, and, although they vary in internal plan, they all include streets, courtyards, room complexes, and large plazas. Some have terraced temple platforms as well. Variations occur in specific plan and in ratio of residence to open space. The largest, Gran Chimu, was probably the palace of the ruler; the others undoubtedly had specialized political or economic functions. The spaces between are crowded with residences, apparently planned and placed within smaller conjoined compounds. Total population of the site is not known, but it was certainly comparable to Teotihuacán or Aztec Tenochtitlan.

Smaller versions of Chan Chan are found in other North Coast valleys, apparently functioning as provincial administrative centers. Other manifestations of a large transvalley state are found in the extensive networks of roads and massive fortifications. Even more impressive evidence is the emergence of huge transvalley canal systems that unite pan-valley systems

---

[16] Rowe, *op. cit.*, pp. 1–27.

into a single master system, the end product of a long history of desert adaptation.

The Inca Empire

The Cuzco Valley, and the Vilcanota drainage system of which it is a part, played a marginal historical role throughout most of Central Andean history. During the Formative and Classic Periods, simple village cultures existed in the valley. During the Early Postclassic, the region enjoyed a brief and ephemeral participation in the more dramatic historical events of Andean history with the establishment of a Wari provincial center and garrison-granary at Pikillakta, but even at that time it was essentially a lightly settled buffer zone between the two great empires. Following the collapse of Wari the region returned to isolation. Occupational remains of the Early Postclassic (Killke phase) are abundant but consist almost entirely of small village sites.

When the Spaniards arrived in Peru in 1532 the situation had changed dramatically. The Vilcanota basin was the demographic and economic heart of a great empire ruled by a dynastic lineage referred to as the *Inca* that stretched from Colombia to central Chile and from the Pacific Ocean to the eastern jungles—the largest political system ever evolved in the New World. The capital of this great empire, Cuzco, was then truly, as the Inca claimed, the "Navel of the World." Although Inca tradition records a list of 13 rulers, their remarkable expansion occurred under the reign of three (Pachacutec, Topa Yupanqui, and Huayna Cápac—father, son, and grandson). Between A.D. 1438 and 1525—a span of only 87 years —they conquered the entire Central Andes and even expanded into neighboring culture areas.

Technologically, the Incas differed little from their predecessors. Inca ceramics and textiles are technically excellent, their metallurgy comparable to the best of Classic and Tiahuanaco work, but none of these crafts witnessed any major innovations in techniques, materials, or functions, nor are the products outstanding in comparison to those of earlier periods. In architecture, however, the Incas were master builders and surpassed all their predecessors in the scale and scope of their constructions.

To state the matter briefly, the Inca continued the Tiahuanaco tradition of dressed and fitted stone masonry but developed a number of distinctive styles adapted to different functions. Regularly coursed small blocks of stone were used for temple and palace constructions; huge polygonal stones, perfectly fitted and joined, were used in construction of terraces for important buildings and fortresses. For less pretentious buildings, cruder coarse masonry, adobe bricks, and mud and split stone walls were used. The basic idea of the compound with rooms arranged around a court was carried over from Tiahuanaco and applied to both palace and temple. State-sponsored building projects included a network of paved roads, suspension bridges of fibre cables, granaries, residences, temples, terrace systems, and hydraulic works. These structures were combined into provincial administrative centers found throughout the empire and are striking architectural testimony to the thoroughness and efficiency of Inca administration.

The empire was centralized in the person of the *Sapa Inca,* or emperor, an absolute ruler. He was served by an army of officials drawn from the royal lineage and the conquered nobility. Inca administration influenced the culture of conquered groups profoundly and included the introduction of the state religion and the Quechua language. As a result, only small areas of non-Quechua language survived until the Spanish conquest, notably Mochica on the North Coast and Áymara in the Titicaca Basin.

Some administrative techniques were approximated by the Aztec, but the Inca carried them out much more extensively and thoroughly. For example, their *mitimae* system involved massive population displacement, organized and sponsored by the state to break up local loyalties and lessen the possibility of revolts. Although the Aztec had a highly organized corvee labor system for construction projects, it was applied primarily to the population of the Basin of Mexico. By way of contrast, the Inca treated their entire giant domain, with a population conservatively estimated at 6,000,000, as a single great labor pool. The Inca state also monopolized production and distribution of goods, and such institutions as the market and merchant guild were almost totally absent. The state also systematically drafted all unusually skilled craftsmen within the empire and forced them to reside at Cuzco to work for the state. Special techniques of administration included a courier system, a complete census of population and resources recorded by the *quipu* (a mnemonic aid consisting of knotted cords representing numbers in a decimal system), and a corps of investigators to observe local officials.

Seven *Marginal Tribes and Chiefdoms*

This chapter summarizes the culture history of marginal tribes and chiefdoms.[1] The groups in question were marginal to the two great civilizations in two respects. First, although agriculture evolved or diffused to these areas at some phase of their history, the consequences of agriculture were tribes and chiefdoms rather than states. Technology was competent and the products aesthetically often impressive, but the latter fell far below the qual-

---

[1] The data for this chapter are drawn primarily from the following sources: Betty J. Meggers and Clifford Evans, eds., *Aboriginal Culture Development in Latin America: An Interpretive Review*, Smithsonian Miscellaneous Collections, vol. 146, no. 1 (Washington: Smithsonian Institution, 1963); Betty J. Meggers, *Ecuador* (New York: Frederick A. Praeger, Inc., 1966); Gerardo Reichel-Dolmatoff, *Colombia* (New York: Frederick A. Praeger, Inc., 1965); Gordon R. Willey, *An Introduction to American Archaeology, Vol. 1: North and Middle America* (Englewood Cliffs, N.J.: Prentice-Hall, Inc., 1966); Jesse Jennings and Edward Norbeck, eds., *Prehistoric Man in the New World* (Chicago: The University of Chicago Press, 1963); James B. Griffin, ed., *Archaeology of the Eastern United States* (Chicago: The University of Chicago Press, 1952); John C. McGregor, *Southwestern Archaeology* (New York: John Wiley & Sons, Inc., 1941); H. M. Wormington, *Prehistoric Indians of the Southwest*, 5th ed., Popular Series No. 7 (Denver: Denver Museum of Natural History, 1961); George I. Quimby, *Indian Life in the Upper Great Lakes, 11,000 B.C. to A.D. 1800* (Chicago: The University of Chicago Press, 1952).

ity of the best Mesoamerican and Central Andean work. Second, the areas were also marginal in a historical sense, with a few notable exceptions, in that a substantial part of the culture was the direct or indirect product of diffusion from the two great centers. Six culture areas are involved: the Intermediate, Caribbean, Tropical Forest, Southern Andes, American Southwest, and Eastern Woodlands.

The Intermediate Area

The Intermediate Area includes the highlands and coastal plain of Ecuador, the highlands and coastal plains of Colombia, and most of Central America. Unlike the other marginal areas it borders on both Mesoamerica and the Central Andes, a critical historical fact. Geographically, the region may be classified under James's complex mountain type, particularly the Colombian and Ecuadorean sectors. The primary characteristic for human adaptation is its microgeographic complexity. Punas, or high-altitude (above 3000 m) grasslands, and high Andean valleys (2000–3000 m) are found primarily in Ecuador, with smaller areas in Colombia. Much of the inhabited parts of the Colombian Andes lies at an intermediate elevation, from 1000 to 2000 m above sea level. This niche is also found on the western escarpment of the Ecuadorean Andes and in a small highland basin in Costa Rica. Most of Central America, the lower escarpment of the Andes, and the coastal plains of Colombia and Ecuador are tropical lowlands. Within these temperature zones is a striking variation in rainfall; generally speaking, however, the Intermediate area has abundant rainfall. There are no extensive areas of desert coastal plain or semiarid highlands, thus contrasting sharply with Mesoamerica and the Central Andes.

The historic culture of the area was characterized by intense sociopolitical fragmentation and great variability, both in ecological adaptation and in specific cultural styles. Combined with this was a rather striking linguistic homogeneity. Chibchan speakers occupied most of Central America and the high Andean valleys around Bogotá. Many languages of highland Ecuador and the Pacific coast of Ecuador have not been classified, but those that have been are all Paezan. Both Paezan and Chibchan are grouped into a Macro-Chibchan phylum by Greenberg.

The Intermediate area is difficult to summarize, in part because of intense stylistic regionalism, in part because of lack of good archaeological data from many local areas. Meggers's scheme for Ecuador (with some changes in dates) will be applied here to the entire area. It includes Early Formative (3000–1000 B.C.), Late Formative (1000–500 B.C.), Regional Development (500 B.C.–A.D. 500) and Integration (A.D. 500 to Contact). The Early Formative has been discussed previously. The Late Formative, although still a period of relatively light population, is characterized by primary dependence on agriculture and expansion of residence from the littoral to inland riparian locations within the tropical lowlands. It is also notable for its stylistic homogeneity. In Colombia the period is represented by the Malambo phase. Malambo pottery shows definite continuities with the preceding Barlovento phase and continues to emphasize plastic decorative techniques. Addition of manioc griddles to the complex is the earliest definite evidence of agriculture in Colombia. The Malambo subsistence pattern was identical with that of historic Amazonian tropical farmers: riverbank root crop cultivation combined with intensive use of river protein foods (turtles were particularly important). A possible counterpart of Malambo in Panama is the Sarigua phase, although griddles and direct evidence of agriculture are absent.

The Chorrera phase on the coastal plain of Ecuador had a historical significance, similar in many ways to Malambo in Colombia. The ceramic complex is a combination of older Machalilla traits with new ones, particularly in the addition of irridescent red-on-base painting and emphasis on highly burnished surfaces. New forms include everted lip and annular base bowls. Other ceramics include hollow and solid handmade figurines, flat stamps, and "napkin ring" earspools. Chorrera is also characterized by heavy use of obsidian tools manufactured by the cylindrical core-blade technique. All these traits are found in the Mesoamerican Middle Formative, and Meggers and Coe [2] have asserted that Chorrera was the product of a Mesoamerican migration. On this basis, and owing to the shift of settlement inland, Meggers argues for introduction of maize from Mesoamerica into Ecuador at this time. The evidence of migration is not very convincing. There is a strong probability that groups in the highlands of Colombia and Ecuador were agricultural at this time and that maize was independently domesticated and introduced from somewhere in the Andes, probably northern Peru, where chiefdoms were well established by 1800 B.C. In summary, both Meggers and Reichel-Dolmatoff have underplayed the role of the North Andean highlands in the early transmission of crops.

Although the Regional Development Period witnessed an explosion of regional styles in almost all ecological niches, within this diversity a number of ceramic traits have widespread distributions, a reflection of the intensive and extensive diffusion characterizing the history of the region. Widely diffused pottery forms include vessels with solid or hollow tripod and polypod feet (including mammiform, conical, and cylindrical forms), pedestal and annular base vessels, spouted and bridged vessels, everted-lip jars, bottles, and open bowls. Distinctive and widespread decorative techniques include polychrome, white-on-red, other bichromes, and negative painting. Other widespread ceramic artifacts include figurines, whistles, masks, spindle whorls, cylindrical and flat stamps, and earspools. Not all are innovations: some appear first in the Early and Late Formative, but in this period they are widely diffused. Not all these traits appear simultaneously in the area as a whole, or in any particular locality.

On the Colombian coast and in Central America, subsistence shifted from an Amázonian type to one based on maize, and in those areas explosive population growth followed. Reichel-Dolmatoff believes that maize was introduced from Mesoamerica and that during the Regional Developmental Period farmers colonized the upland regions in Colombia. Again, another interpretation can be offered: that maize diffused north through the North Andean highlands (from the Central Andes) and reached coastal

---

[2] Meggers, *Ecuador*; and Michael D. Coe, "Archaeological Linkages with North and South America at La Victoria, Guatemala," *American Anthropologist*, vol. 62 (1960), pp. 363–393.

Ecuador by 1000 B.C. and the Caribbean coast of Colombia a few centuries before Christ.

Regardless of how the question of the ultimate origin of maize in South America will be resolved, there is ample evidence for establishment of the historic subsistence pattern of the Intermediate area by A.D. 1. Agriculture was probably extensive, involving various types of swidden. Most sites indicated for the period are small villages. Burials, houses, and artifacts do not indicate great variation in social status, and large civic or residential centers are absent. In other words, the societal level was probably tribal.

A major exception is in a nearly continuous territory that includes the north coast of Ecuador, the adjacent coastal plain in Colombia, and the South Andean highlands of Colombia, where unusually complex cultures flourished. La Tolita, for example, in Esmeraldas Province, Ecuador, is a large site with at least 40 artificial earth mounds. The highest mound is 9 m. high and has a flat, rectangular surface area of 20×45 m. Another flat-topped, rectangular mound was 2 m high and covered an area 25×82 m. Several mounds, including the highest, were grouped around a plaza 192 m square. Looting has produced enormous quantities of ceramic figurines and pottery; the former represent one of the New World's great artistic traditions. Other ceramics include masks, stamps, effigy whistles, flutes, panpipes, and spindle whorls. Many of them, including the figurines, are mold-made. Figurines cover a wide range: some are of elaborately costumed men, sometimes dressed in bird or jaguar headgear; others represent a variety of creatures: felines, reptiles, snakes, birds; still others have movable arms and legs; others represent gods, and several are of considerable historical interest—old men with deeply wrinkled faces, dual-faced beings, and alter-ego beings (a large figure with a smaller one perched on the head, neck, or shoulders). A series of C14 dates from sites in Colombia range from 400 B.C. to A.D. 200.

Another elaborate manifestation of the period is found at San Agustín, 1700 m above sea level in southern Colombia. Over 30 major sites of the San Agustín culture are known. These include civic centers composed of earth funerary mounds, with interior stone slab galleries and tombs. Though not as well constructed, they resemble the Castillo of Chavín. Within the tombs are carved sarcophagi. These centers seem not to have large attached residential areas. The population was dispersed in hamlets. Another distinctive status burial found in the area is represented by deep-shaft tombs. A distinctive feature of San Agustín culture is stone sculpture, some of it in the form of relief carvings on boulders or cliff faces, others in the form of columnar statues. The latter vary in skill of carving, but the best do not approach Mesoamerican or Central Andean standards. Distinctive motifs are humans shown with fangs and mouths very similar to Chavín style; hybrid human–feline figures, the alter-ego motif, and humans carrying clubs or playing panpipes. Many elaborate manifestations of San Agustín apparently appeared during the Integration Period. Representative features of the culture definitely ascribed to the Regional Developmental Phase are the deep shaft-graves and beaten gold jewelry. The earth mounds and stone sculpture apparently date from the later period. Duque Gomez [3] suggests

---

[3] See Carlos Valdes, "Cultural Development in Colombia," in Meggers and Evans, *op. cit.*, pp. 55–66.

that sculptural themes seen in stone in the Integration Period were expressed in wood during earlier times.

The Regional Development Period, in summary, was one in which sedentary village life became established over the entire region (except, perhaps, the high Andean villages around Bogotá). It was a period of intensive and extensive primary diffusion, one in which chiefdoms emerged in one small sector that included both lowland and highland niches. The close similarity of themes in the art of the chiefdoms to those in Formative art of the Central Andes and Mesoamerica, and the sharing of a great number of fairly specialized ceramic forms and decorative techniques with those two areas, indicates that they were probably in direct contact with the two civilizations.

We are less resistant to the idea of direct contact at this time for a variety of reasons: first, the evidence of contact in the artifacts themselves seems more convincing. Second, during the Regional Development Period in Ecuador the social environment in Mesoamerica was much more conducive to contacts, either by migration or by trade. Most of central and southern Mesoamerica was occupied by large chiefdoms and states engaged in intense competition. This competition could easily have dislodged a small chiefdom and forced the population to move. There is some linguistic support for this thesis: the historic population of Esmeraldas Province spoke a language related to Jicaque and Subtiaba in Honduras and Nicaragua, and all belong to the Hokan-Siouan family.[4] Conceivably, the specific influences noted, as well as the linguistic similarities, could have been the product of colonizing merchants and trade; but the distances are too great, and New World sea travel was too primitive for the maintenance of regularized trade. More probably, an expulsion and permanent migration was the mechanism. For Central Andean influences, the distances involved are much less, and these influences were probably the product of coastal trade organized by the large chiefdoms and small states of the North Peruvian coast. The Esmeraldas chiefdoms were very likely the main agents in diffusion of both Mesoamerican and Central Andean traits to inland areas.

The Integration Period was essentially characterized by the appearance of chiefdoms throughout the region. It was also a period of fewer, more widely distributed regional styles and of the appearance of centers comparable in size to Late Formative Centers in Mesoamerica. This generalization is more applicable to Ecuador than to Colombia or Central America. In these last two regions tribes remained sandwiched in between the chiefdoms (particularly in the tropical lowlands) until the historic period. Incipient states may have emerged in Ecuador toward the end of the period. All over the Intermediate area the Integration Period was one of maximum population; not only were the high valleys around Bogotá densely settled, but the largest chiefdoms in Colombia were located there. It was a period of specialized ecological adaptations including integral swidden and swamp reclamation (in the form of ridge and ditch systems) in the lowlands, and terracing, contour hoeing, and small-scale irrigation in the highlands.

Technologically, the major new development was a great elaboration of

---

[4] Julian H. Steward and Louis C. Faron, *Native Peoples of South America* (New York: McGraw-Hill Book Company, 1959), pp. 22–23.

metallurgy, which utilized most of the Central Andean techniques and undoubtedly derived from that area. It was from the Central American sector of the area that Mesoamerica received the fundamental techniques of metallurgy. Public construction, utilizing earth and stone, included temples and elite residences, but major architectural efforts were expressed in tombs. Stone sculpture was widely but spottily distributed. Important centers were at San Agustín in Colombia, the Mánabi Coast in Ecuador, and several areas in Central America. A common motif is the alter-ego.

Tropical Forest— Caribbean Farmers

The vast region east of the Andes and north of the Pampas was occupied in historic times by a thinly scattered population. In Chapter Two the historic cultures were classified into three types with respect to subsistence patterns: hunters and gatherers, incipient cultivators, and tropical forest farmers. There is ethnographic evidence that the incipient cultivators were hunters and gatherers until a few centuries before Contact. They were found mostly in rugged headwaters or savanna country. The tropical farmers had a distribution correlated closely with forest areas, and within such environments residence was strikingly littoral or riparian. Both types emphasized root cultivation, primarily manioc, but the tropical farmers also had a subsistence focus on river protein resources. A highly specialized variant of manioc cultivation, involving use of bitter manioc (from which the poisonous juices were removed by basketry presses and the dry pulp processed into griddle cakes) was found among groups residing along the Middle and Lower Amazon, the lower reaches of its major tributaries, within the Orinoco drainage, and in the Antilles.

The hunters and gatherers were organized in bands, incipient cultivators and tropical farmers primarily in tribes. Chiefdoms were found in a few widely spaced areas; eastern Bolivia, along the Middle and Lower Amazon, on the coast of Venezuela, and in the Greater Antilles. Most hunters and gatherers and incipient cultivators were Macro-Ge speakers; with exception of the Carib, the majority of tropical farmers were either Tupi-Guaraní or Arawak speakers, both groups being members of the Equatorial phylum. Both Tupi-Guaraní and Arawak shared the Amazon Basin, the former tending to have a southern, the latter a northern, distribution.

These ethnographic facts of the area have been repeated since they immediately suggest major historical problems as well as solutions. The major problems relate to the origin of agriculture in general, the origin and history of the various types of subsistence, the relationship of linguistic distributions to these problems, and the processes that led to the historical distribution of societal types.

Concerning the origin of agriculture, the basic question is whether it was an independent development or else the product of indirect or direct diffusion from the Andes. The Tropical Forest region extends along the eastern edge of the Andes for 2000 km. Agriculture was well established over the latter region by 1000 B.C., and the great network of rivers provided ready access to tropical lowlands along the entire length of the "diffusion rim." With respect to specialized forms of tropical agriculture, particularly the bitter manioc dietary complex, there is no question of their origin in the tropical lowlands. The major problems are those of place, date, and processes that led to their evolution and diffusion. The most detailed archaeological data are from Venezuela and the Antilles, where Rouse[5] and Cruxent[6] have provided a wealth of information. Most of Venezuela was occupied by Arawak speakers in historic times. They were organized in chiefdoms on the Caribbean coast and in the Venezuelan Andes, and in tribal societies along the Orinoco River system.

Ceramics, and possibly incipient cultivation of manioc, may have appeared first in the arid coastal plain around Lake Maracaibo at some time between 2700 and 300 B.C.; however, the earliest definite evidence of manioc cultivation is from the Lower Orinoco (approximately 1000 B.C.). The cultures in question (the Saladoid and Barrancoid traditions) are associated with small village sites situated along the river. Apparently the bitter manioc dietary complex had already evolved, since pottery manioc griddles are present; they are particularly common on sites of the Barrancoid ceramic tradition, which has close stylistic similarities to Malambo in Colombia. Manioc may have been introduced, possibly by migration, from Colombia. At any rate, conflicts between Barrancoid and Saladoid groups led to a series of local migrations: one Saladoid group moved upstream to the Middle Orinoco; the other moved to the coast, where they appear to have absorbed the older Manicuaroid littoral gatherers.

At about the time of Christ, some coastal Saladoid groups colonized the Lesser Antilles. Subsequent history of the Antilles is one of gradual population expansion and colonization of the larger islands by tropical forest farmers at the expense of native food gatherers. Puerto Rico was occupied by A.D. 200, Hispaniola and Jamaica by A.D. 700, and Cuba a century later. All sites in the Antilles and in Venezuela up to about A.D. 1000 were small agricultural villages. Between A.D. 1000 and 1500 chiefdoms emerged in the larger Antillean islands, along the Venezuela coast, and in the Venezuela Andes.

Most of these population movements probably involved Arawak speakers. If introduction of Barrancoid ceramics was the product of migration from Colombia, the migrants may have been ancestors of the Warrau, a Paezan-speaking group residing in the Orinoco delta in historic times. A few centuries before the conquest, Carib speakers (of the Macro-Ge super-phylum) residing in interior Guiana adopted agriculture and embarked on a series of migrations as far afield as Colombia, Venezuela, the Amazon Basin, and the Lesser Antilles.

Archaeological data from the Amazon Basin are extremely scanty. Evans[7] has postulated four stages of culture history: Hunting and Gathering, Incipient Agriculture, Tropical Forest Slash-and-Burn Farming, and Sub-Andean. Sites of the second stage have been reported on the Lower

---

[5] Irving Rouse, "Prehistory of the West Indies," *Science*, vol. 144, no. 3618 (1964).

[6] Jose Cruxent and Irving Rouse, "Venezuela and Its Relationship with Neighboring Areas," *Actas del XXXIII Congreso Internacional de Americanistas, San Jose, 1958* (San Jose, Costa Rica, 1959), I, pp. 173–182.

[7] Clifford Evans, "Lowland South America," in Jennings and Norbeck, *op. cit.*, pp. 419–450.

Amazon (in one case a shell midden), eastern Ecuador, and eastern Peru. All consist of small villages, have pottery, but lack manioc griddles. Since milling stones are also absent, the basic crop (if agriculture was practiced at all) must have been a root crop. Although local ceramics differ in detail, all share a characteristic zoned hachure and incised design. Evans dates the stage between 1000 B.C. and A.D. 1 and suggests that it was produced by downriver migration from the Andes foothills.

During the Tropical Forest Stage (A.D. 1–Contact) villages became larger and were apparently abandoned on an average of every two generations as extensive swidden cultivation used up nearby primary forest. Sites are reported on the Amazon, along several of its major tributaries, and in the Upper Orinoco Basin. The ceramics have been grouped in two horizon styles, an Incised Rim Horizon (A.D. 1–800) and an Incised Punctate Horizon (A.D. 1000–1500). It should be noted that neither is a genuine horizon style in the Central Andean sense. Evans ascribes the distribution of each to periodic migrations but does not specify sources.

There is stylistic evidence that during the Incised Rim Horizon, groups migrated to the Upper Orinoco in the 8th century A.D. Influences from the immigrants transformed the Middle Orinoco Saladoid culture and a new culture—Arauquinoid—emerged around A.D. 1000, bearing remarkably expansive qualities. These contacts between Amazonian and Orinoco groups were historically important, since the manioc griddle appears suddenly in the Amazon Basin during the Incised-Punctate Horizon and its rapid diffusion was undoubtedly the result of these contacts.

Between A.D. 1000 and 1300 a number of groups with more elaborate culture, including polychrome ceramics and burial mounds, migrated downriver from Ecuador to Marajó Island in the Amazon delta. Evans refers to this event as the Sub-Andean Stage.

The history of the Plata drainage basin and the east coast of Brazil seems to recapitulate the processes already described for the Amazon. Ethnohistoric documentation of migrations is particularly detailed. Most historic tropical forest farmers spoke Tupi-Guaraní. Archaeology and ethnohistory indicate that Tupi-Guaraní groups moved from the Lower Amazon into the Upper Paraná between A.D. 800 and 1000, expanded first to the South Brazilian Coast by 1000, and then northward along the coast. This northward coastal movement was still underway when the Europeans arrived. The Tupi-Guaraní introduced the Tropical Forest pattern to the region. The absence of the bitter manioc complex in historic times was due to the fact that the migration preceded its appearance in the Amazon. Over most of the area they traveled, the Tupi-Guaraní encountered hunting and gathering Ge speakers, but in the Chaco they were apparently preceded by incipient cultivators. The ceramics of the earlier group are referred to as the Punctate-Incised Ceramic tradition.

In summary, archaeology of the tropical lowlands, scanty as it is, suggests initial introduction of agriculture from the Andean foothills during the first millennium B.C. The bitter manioc culinary complex apparently originated in the Caribbean lowlands and diffused very late into the Amazon Basin. Archaeological data support the idea that much of the diffusion in the area was the product of population movement. One is tempted to relate this to an expansion of Tupi-Guaraní and Arawak speakers.

Farmers of the Southern Andes

Archaeological data from the Southern Andes is limited to the more arid northern portions of the area, northwestern Argentina, and northern Chile. We have no data on the history of central Argentina or the Araucanian area of central Chile. Linguistically and culturally the north, in historic times, was simple; it is thus relatively easy to summarize.

The Atacameño (Macro-Chibchan speakers) occupied northern Chile; the Diaguita (of unknown linguistic affiliation) occupied northwestern Argentina. The culture was essentially one of tribal farmers having adapted to an arid environment; variations in culture were primarily the result of variations in water resources. The major historical problems are two: definition of the history of this dry land adaptation and definition of the role of the Central Andes in its history. With respect to the latter problem it would be useful briefly to summarize the history of the nearby Bolivian Plateau.

The Titicaca Basin was occupied by sedentary farmers around 1000 B.C.; a few centuries before Christ the first elaborate culture emerged at Tiahuanaco. Between A.D. 1 and 800 Tiahuanaco evolved into a major Andean center. Contemporary with its development were a series of local cultures south of La Paz that shared such traits as monochrome pottery, metallurgy, and funerary mounds and that were subsumed under the heading of "Megalithic Culture" by Bolivian archaeologists. Between A.D. 800 and 1200 Tiahuanaco politically dominated the Bolivian and south Peruvian Andes; between A.D. 1200 and 1450 a cultural regression appeared over the region, urban life disappeared, and a phase of political fragmentation followed. After 1450 the region fell under political control of the Inca.

The history of the Southern Andes may be summarized in four periods: Early Ceramic (200 B.C.–A.D. 800), Middle Ceramic (A.D. 800–1200), Late Ceramic (A.D. 1200–1450), and Inca (A.D. 1450–Contact).[8] Agriculture, ceramics, loom weaving, animal domestication, and metallurgy all enter the area simultaneously sometime between 500 and 200 B.C. The crops (potatoes, maize, quinoa), farming techniques (irrigation, terracing), domestic animals (llamas, alpacas), ceramics, weaving, and metallurgical techniques are all Central Andean in derivation. The influence was apparently by diffusion, rather than through actual migration. Between 200 B.C. and A.D. 200 a number of distinct regional monochrome styles were present; between A.D. 200 and 800 a variety of polychrome styles appear along with such specific coastal Central Andean forms as stirrup- and bridge-spouted vessels and such characteristic techniques of ceramic decoration as negative painting. These influences may have involved actual population movements from the tiny far south coast valleys of Peru. The local settlement pattern of the period consisted of small villages of scattered stone houses.

---

[8] Alberto R. Gonzalez, "Cultural Development in Northwestern Argentina," in Meggers and Evans, *op. cit.*, pp. 103–118. More recent versions of Central Andean chronology would place Gonzalez's Middle Period between A.D. 800–1200 with corresponding changes in the preceding and succeeding phases, so his absolute dates are here modified.

The Middle Period witnessed an intensification of influences from the Central Andes, now from Tiahuanaco. An actual Tiahuanaco colony was established in the Atacameño area; outside this, the influence was variable, indirect, and probably the product of trade—perhaps with the colony. One of the local regions, the Valliserrano, came under notably heavy influence, and the resultant culture is elaborate enough to represent a chiefdom structure. Distinctive features included a religious cult focused on a feline god and an elaborately costumed warrior deity. Tiahuanaco influence is reflected in polychrome ceramics, bronze metallurgy, and stone sculpture. Burials indicate a definite ranking principle in Valliserrano society, but settlement patterns remain unchanged.

During the Late Ceramic Period there was a striking artistic decline, though metallurgy reached a climactic development. Particularly character-istic are widely traded bells and elaborate ceremonial axes. Another in-novation was replacement of the spear by the bow. Sites are considerably larger, consisting of large, conjoined, multi-roomed villages, some with an extension of up to 16 ha; hilltop fortresses of stone are also found. The custom of elaborate funerary offerings and cults of the warrior and feline gods vanished. In the reign of the invincible Topa Inca Yupanqui (A.D. 1471–93) the entire northwestern Argentina region and northern half of Chile were incorporated into the Inca empire; evidence of the conquest is direct and abundant in the form of roads, forts, administrative centers, and ceramics.

Desert Cultivators
of the Southwest

By approximately 3000 B.C. a number of cultures of the Desert Hunting and Gathering tradition were present in the southwestern part of the United States. One local culture was Cochise, located in the Mogollon Mountains of southeastern Arizona and southwestern New Mexico. The Mogollon is a semiarid low mountain region, less arid than the lower-lying Gila Basin to the south, the Rio Grande Valley to the east, and the Colorado Plateau to the north. Sometime between 3000 and 2000 B.C. maize was introduced in the area, the earliest known north of Mexico.

The sites are in dry upland valleys in ecological niches similar to those of sites of early plant domestication in Mesoamerica. By 1000 B.C. squash and beans were added, completing the North American crop trilogy. The maize was a small-eared variety of low productivity. Its introduction altered the life way of the Cochise collectors only slightly. Apparently local evolution of the plant, combined with hybridization of new varieties introduced from the south, permitted the achievement of sedentary village life in the Mogollon by 300 B.C. Sites consisted of small pit-house villages. Also making its first appearance was pottery, a red-slipped ware in the form of hemispherical bowls, jars, and tecomates. Between 100 B.C. and A.D. 400 this new pattern of life, with its primary dependence on agriculture, pit houses, and ceramics, gradually diffused to surrounding areas. After A.D. 400 regional differentiation characterizes the culture history. There were four major cultural traditions:

Patayan on the Colorado, Anasazi on the Colorado Plateau, Hohokam in the Gila River Basin, and Mogollon in the Mogollon Mountains. The Mogollon was relatively static, and few changes occurred within it until the Anasazi absorption in the final prehistoric phases. The others ultimately evolved into the three types of historic farming cultures in the area, the Yuman, Pima, and Pueblo respectively.

The history of the Anasazi tradition has been segmented into six phases. The earliest, Basketmaker II (100 B.C.–A.D. 400), lacks pottery. A distinctive feature of the culture is coiled basketry and garments woven from yucca fibre. Also present were spear-throwers and darts (the latter with chipped stone notched-base points), and milling stones, basic tools of the Desert Hunters and Gatherers. Added to this were agriculture and villages (up to 50 houses, but most villages were of lineage size) of substantial pit houses of timber and earth. In each village at least one pit house had ceremonial functions comparable to the Kiva, the historic Anasazi fraternity house. Other innovations included full-grooved axes and tubular stone pipes. In the succeeding Basketmaker III phase (A.D. 400–700) pottery, painted in the characteristic Anasazi black-on-white technique, was added to the tradition. Towards the end of the phase, the bow, loom weaving of cotton cloth, and domestic turkeys appear.

The succeeding Pueblo I phase (A.D. 700–900) was essentially a transitional phase between the Basketmaker and fully developed Anasazi culture. The major change was a shift from pit houses to residence in conjoined rectangular rooms constructed of wattle and daub. The pit house was retained as a Kiva. Villages remained small, up to 50 rooms, and were probably occupied by one lineage or, at the most, by several. Basketry and yucca fibre textiles declined as pottery and cotton cloth became more popular; the bow replaced the spear-thrower and spear, and ceramics became highly elaborated in form and design. In Pueblo II times, the major technological change was from wattle-and-daub walls to stone wall construction. A significant change occurred in the settlement pattern: this was dispersal to very small settlements, each of a few conjoined rooms with a Kiva; some are so small that they were probably occupied by extended families.

The Pueblo III phase (A.D. 1100–1300) has often been called the Great Period. It was the phase of maximum geographic extension of the culture, and also of elaboration of ceramics and stone architecture. The population resided in large, planned, terraced, multiroomed apartment house-villages, the historic Anasazi nucleated tribe. One of these, Pueblo Bonito, had 800 rooms. Pueblo III villages offered blank walls to the outside world and were natural forts. Many villages were also constructed on defensive sites, within rock shelters on sheer-rock faces, on the flat summits, or on steep-sided mesas. There is convincing evidence that the process of nucleation was a defensive measure. Most archaeologists have blamed warlike nomads, and many have nominated the historic Apache, but it is more likely that the conflicts were among the Pueblo themselves. The first definite evidence of intensive farming practices—in the form of irrigation canals, checkdams, and terraces—dates from this period. Between A.D. 1275 and 1300, the Anasazi suffered a striking reduction of geographic range and massive population displacements. Most of the population moved to the Rio Grande

Valley, where the Spaniards found them in the 16th century living in large adobe villages. The final phase of Anasazi history is known as Pueblo IV (A.D. 1300–1700).

Contrasting sharply with the Anasazi is the Hohokam tradition in the Gila River Basin. The history has been divided into the following phases: Pioneer (100 B.C.–A.D. 500), Colonial (A.D. 500–900), Sedentary (A.D. 900–1200), and Classic (A.D. 1200–1400). Basic Hohokam culture was well established in the Pioneer phase; subsequent changes up to A.D. 1200 represent minor additions. Subsistence was based on irrigation agriculture with great canal systems. Residence was in small villages of wattle-and-daub houses with depressed floors. Other characteristics included red-on-buff painted pottery, pottery figurines, three-quarter grooved axes, cotton weaving, shell jewelry, ground and polished stone palettes, and bowls. All these features were present in the Pioneer phase and persisted throughout Hohokam history with the usual stylistic variations. The spear and spear-thrower were in use during the Pioneer phase, to be replaced by the bow in the later phases. Ball courts appeared during the Colonial phase; small, low, earth platforms, comparable in form and function to the temple platform of Mesoamerica, and cast copper bells (apparently imported from Mexico) are both present during the Sedentary phase.

The Classic phase witnessed striking changes in settlement patterns, in part produced by Anasazi immigration. The two groups lived side by side in the same villages, each preserving its own culture. Villages consisted of great adobe compounds—in some cases a number of them—within which were Hohokam-type houses and adobe apartment houses of the Anasazi type. Within the same village each type of house contained the typical ceramics, artifacts, and burials of the respective ethnic groups, a remarkable example of peaceful coexistence. Ultimately, the Anasazi immigrants abandoned the area, as did most Hohokam. The final prehistoric phase is poorly defined, but historic Pima apparently represent the end of the tradition. The major factor that produced the exodus was the drying up of irrigation water sources.

Prehistoric antecedents of the historic Yumans, flood-plain cultivators of the Colorado, are found in the Patayan tradition. Around A.D. 600 the local Desert Collectors received, apparently from the Hohokam, maize, beans, squash, pottery, and wattle-and-daub houses. Subsequent internal changes within the tradition were changes of style. The culture was subject to continuous influences from Hohokam and generally looks like a degraded version of that tradition, with such elaborations as ball courts, platform mounds, metallurgy, carved stone bowls, and shell ornaments all absent or only slightly developed.

The history of the Southwest, like that of the Southern Andes, is essentially one of a farming population adapting to a marginal and arid frontier. Water resources were scanty and scattered; total population was small and concentrated in widely spaced, intensively utilized pockets. Although technological and subsistence features from Mesoamerica were significant in shaping the history of the area, the cultures were highly parochial and can best be understood in terms of local processes. Tribal societies were probably present by Basketmaker II times. Subsequent history was one of increasingly larger and better-organized tribes. There are few if any hints of more complex social systems.

Cultivators
of the Eastern Woodlands

The Eastern Woodlands were occupied in the historic period by a thinly distributed, tribally organized population with subsistence based on extensive swidden cultivation combined with hunting and gathering. The majority of specialists in eastern archaeology feel that this had always been true. We agree only in part with this evaluation and believe that the archaeology shows evidence of a denser population than has been conceded, a density achieved through intensive cultivation of river floodplains. There is also some evidence of a much wider distribution of chiefdoms in the century or two prior to Contact. In this section we will first summarize the archaeological data and then discuss the pros and cons of these points of view.

In approximately 1000 B.C. a series of striking technological and economic changes occurred in Eastern Woodland culture that ultimately transformed the old Archaic lifeway. Major innovations were agriculture, the elaboration of funerary ritual (including construction of large, conical, earth burial mounds) and pottery. Pottery did appear first on the Georgia coast in Late Archaic times, but it remained a spatially restricted, historically isolated phenomenon.

Between 1000 and 300 B.C. these three traits spread gradually but unevenly over the Eastern Woodlands. Burial mounds remained restricted to the Central Mississippi and Ohio Valley, ceramics did not appear in the Lower Mississippi Valley and Gulf Coast until the end of the period, and many groups remained nonagricultural. The period has been referred to as Burial Mound I after the impressive funerary architecture.

The overall picture with respect to agriculture is somewhat obscure. Caldwell[9] has argued that agriculture, if present at all, was of little significance, and that Burial Mound I and even succeeding Burial Mound II cultures were simply elaborations of the old Archaic lifeway. Griffin[10] and Willey,[11] on the other hand, insist that large mounds imply an agricultural subsistence base. Direct evidence of tropical cultigens in Burial Mound I times is limited to several varieties of cucurbits found in rock shelters in Kentucky. Excavations in many sites in the area of heaviest concentration of burial mounds (and presumably the area of heaviest population) have revealed storage caches of sunflower, marsh elder, and chenopodium seeds (all native plants cultivated by the historic Indians). There is a strong possibility of an independent center of plant domestication in the eastern United States, and this interpretation is favored here. The archaeological

---

[9] J. R. Caldwell, *Trend and Tradition in the Prehistory of the Eastern United States*, Memoir 88 (Menasha, Wisc.: American Anthropological Association, 1958).

[10] James B. Griffin, "Eastern North American Archaeology: A Summary," *Science*, vol. 156 (1967), pp. 175–192.

[11] Willey, *op. cit.*, pp. 267–268.

data suggest that agriculture, ceramics, and burial mounds emerged first in the Ohio and Middle Mississippi valleys and gradually diffused from that center. At least four major regional ceramic traditions emerged by the end of the period.

Northeastern pottery was manufactured with a cord-wrapped paddle and had a characteristic cord-impressed surface. On the South Atlantic Coast and adjacent inland areas designs were impressed on the surface by carved wooden paddles. In Tennessee and Kentucky pottery was decorated with fabric impressions, whereas the population of the Lower Mississippi Valley and adjacent Gulf Coast used incision, punctation, and painting. Caldwell [12] refers to these four traditions as Northern, Appalachian, Fabric-Impressed, and Gulf respectively. Within these major traditions local stylistic diversity was considerable, and there was much interchange of style and technique. However, the pattern of diffusion of ceramics, agriculture, and funerary practices does not suggest major population movements or political expansion. Sites in the core area consist of clusters of burial mounds as ritual centers for a sustaining population dispersed in hamlets of pole and bark houses. Besides pottery, residential sites include a variety of chipped and ground stone tools comparable to those of the Late Archaic, with only minor changes. A new development is an elaboration of bodily ornaments fashioned from antler, bone, stone, and beaten copper. Many of these were manufactured specifically for burial.

This cultural pattern reached its climactic development in the succeeding Burial Mound II Period (300 B.C.–A.D. 700). Two developments—the diffusion of burial mounds, pottery, and agriculture over most of the culture area, and evolution and wide diffusion of a spectacular local style called Hopewell—characterize the period. Evidence of maize cultivation also appears. The demographic and cultural center of the period was the Scioto River Valley in Ohio. The Ohio Hopewell culture rivaled the Formative cultures of Mesoamerica and the Central Andes. Major centers such as the Newark Works include huge circular, rectangular, and octagonal earth enclosures, some adjoining, and others connected by great processional avenues flanked by earth banks. The walls were pierced by gateways. Some enclosures measure more than 40 ha and have walls 5 m high. Associated are clusters of burial mounds and residences, although most of the population continued to reside in hamlets. Burial ritual was extremely complex: sacred enclosures of poles were erected on ground level, within which were special buildings that housed crematories, log tombs, and storehouses for offerings. Grave furniture was abundant, including mica and sheet copper cutouts, freshwater pearls, copper panpipes, polished stone and ceramic earplugs sheathed in copper, elaborately carved polished-stone spear-thrower weights, pottery vessels, and great caches of obsidian artifacts and chipped chert discs. Following a series of rituals and numerous burials the entire enclosure was covered by a conical earth mound. An extensive trading network existed through which the Hopewellian craftsmen obtained raw materials and exported finished products. Hopewellian artifacts were widely traded and imitated over much of the east.

Between A.D. 500 and 1000 the specific Hopewellian artifact style and

---

[12] Caldwell, *op. cit.*

tradition disappeared, the extensive trade network broke down, the elaborate funerary cult declined, and the artistic quality of craft products deteriorated. Parallel to this decline a new cultural tradition was emerging in some areas of the East that was ultimately to replace the Burial Mound way of life; this was the Mississippian. It is defined by the following elements: construction of large, terraced, earth platforms grouped around plazas and serving as sub-structures for temples, elite residences, and council buildings; a tendency for settlements to occur on or immediately above the floodplains of major rivers; a much greater reliance on agriculture, now based on maize, beans, and squash; and wide diffusion of a number of ceramic forms and techniques of decoration, some new, others derived from the Gulf and Northern traditions. Settlement patterns were of two types; large, compact, stockaded villages directly associated with civic centers, and dispersed settlements loosely clustered in the vicinity of centers.

Within the Mississippian, archaeologists have defined several regional stylistic traditions; the total period during which these flourished is referred to as the Temple Mound Period. The most vigorous and expansive of these styles is referred to as Middle Mississippian and seems to have originated somewhere near the confluence of the Mississippi, Missouri, and Ohio rivers between A.D. 700 and 1000, perhaps at the huge Cahokia site. The style ultimately spread over most of the Central Mississippi, Lower Ohio, Tennessee-Cumberland, and Arkansas river valleys, and outliers are reported as far afield as Wisconsin, Georgia, and Alabama. In several cases there is definite evidence that colonization was involved. Some of the Mississippian regional styles evolved as the product of contacts between invaders and the local population. By the 16th century the Mississippianization of the east was far advanced, and large civic centers were found at Cahokia, Illinois; Moundville, Alabama; Spiro, Oklahoma; Coles Creek, Louisiana; and Etowah, Georgia. Technological innovations were slight, elbow pipes replaced platform and tubular pipes, and the bow replaced the spear and spear-thrower. A distinctive Mississippian artifact is a small triangular arrowpoint.

A striking phenomenon of the later phases of the Temple Mound Period was diffusion of a religious system that has been referred to as the Southern Death Cult. It included as major symbols a weeping or winged eye, the cross, sun circles, bilobate arrows, human hands with eyes or crosses on the palm, human skulls, long bones, and dancing men in elaborate costumes; also characteristic were animal symbols, particularly eagles, and feline and feathered serpents. The various symbols are found on shell and copper ornaments and on pottery. These objects occur in status burials associated with polished stone batons, celts, and beautifully chipped flint daggers. At Etowah each burial contained one or more of these objects, suggesting that they were insignia of specific status positions. The cult objects are found primarily at major centers, and their distribution disregards completely the boundaries of stylistic regions.

Many of the groups that shared in the Middle Mississippian tradition, together with contemporary groups in the Lower Mississippi Valley and Gulf Coast, were probably organized into chiefdoms. It is doubtful whether tribes are capable of building Monk's Mound at Cahokia (a huge temple platform 30 m high and with a basal area of 6 ha) or even the much smaller civic centers of Moundville or Etowah. The major Eastern Woodland sites are comparable in scale to the largest Formative sites in Mesoamerica or the Central Andes. Evidence from Mississippian burials is further indication of a wide range of social status. Even more convincing is the presence of large chiefdoms associated with the Temple Mound cult at the time of Contact. The restricted distribution of chiefdoms in historic times may be a result of the spread of disease accompanying the arrival of the Europeans. When the French arrived in the Central Mississippi Valley they found a sparse population, although this was the demographic heartland in Temple Mound times.

During the Burial Mound Period most groups were probably tribally organized. The majority of the burial mounds are small and were apparently used by the entire population. In two areas, however, chiefdom social structure may have been present. In the Scioto Valley Hopewellian sites are comparable in size to the largest Mississippi sites, and there is evidence of status differentiation in burials. Most Hopewellians were interred in hamlets, with mound burial reserved for the elite group. The sorting of burials into log tombs and cremations within the mounds strongly suggests burials of chiefs and retainers. The quality of grave-goods appears as the work of craftsmen attached to chiefly households. Furthermore, the extensive, centralized trade network could not have been maintained by tribally organized populations. The Weeden Island culture of the Gulf Coast may also have had a chiefdom social structure; there the burial mounds were constructed in a single ceremony that included central interment of one individual wearing elaborate beaten copper and shell ornaments, accompanied by human sacrifices and abundant grave offerings.

A common topic in Eastern archaeology is the role of Mesoamerican influences in the development of Eastern Woodland culture, and there is a wide range of opinion on the subject. Some writers explain much of Eastern Woodland history as the product of periodic direct or indirect contacts; others see the history as essentially one of local evolution.

There is little doubt the major agricultural crops were ultimately derived from Mexico, but there is a possibility that they arrived indirectly by way of the Southwest. Some archaeologists have argued that the Burial Mound Cult, ceramics generally, and specific ceramic modes derive from Mesoamerican influence, possibly introduced by migration but more probably by trade. The cultural resemblances are not specific, and no Mesoamerican trade objects have been found in any Burial Mound site. The ceramic similarities are in isolated traits, not style complexes.

The arguments are stronger with respect to the factors that led to the evolution of the Mississippi Temple Mound, which resembles very closely its Mesoamerican counterpart in construction, function, and arrangement into plaza complexes. There are striking resemblances in Mississippian pottery to certain Mesoamerican pottery complexes, but unfortunately for the diffusionist position—and of considerable interest with respect to principles of stylistic evolution—the resemblances are to the Mesoamerican Middle Formative! Finally, there are no reported Mesoamerican trade objects from any Mississippian site, nor did any specific Mississippian ceramic complex reproduce in total any Mesoamerican complex. The strongest argument for direct ties between the two areas is the Southern Death Cult; the symbols are very close to those found in the contemporary Postclassic religious art of Mexico: solar and feathered serpent symbols combined with the symbols of human sacrifice.

The diffusion of the cult could have been the product of a group of traveling merchants like the Aztec Pochteca. The latter were a tough, aggressive, aristocratically organized group, perfectly capable of conducting such long-range trading expeditions. Furthermore, they frequently settled among, and politically dominated, local populations. The kinds of culture traits in Temple Mound culture that look Mesoamerican are precisely those that the Pochteca would be likely to introduce: religious concepts, notions about rank, and specific sumptuary practices, such as human sacrifice. Furthermore, the Pochteca would be attracted to major population centers, and the tendency of the cult to ignore ethnic (*i.e.* sylistic) boundaries would thus be explained. In this case the absence of many Mesoamerican traits in the Temple Mound culture (such as writing, the calendar, and true metallurgy) does not preclude this reconstruction. Postclassic Mesoamerican society was characterized by intense specialization; the Pochteca themselves would not be familiar with details of astrological and craft skills that were the province of other specialists.

This mechanism of diffusion conceivably explains Mesoamerican influences on earlier time horizons as well, at least from Early Classic times onward, when cultures of a social complexity comparable to historic Aztec were present in Mesoamerica.

Eight New World Culture History

In Chapter One some of the basic theories of cultural dynamics were discussed. In the succeeding six chapters a brief summary of New World culture history was presented, the *when* and *where* of development of native cultures. In this chapter an attempt will be made to apply the theoretical principles to the *how* and *why* of that history.

Cultures change in two essential steps: innovation, followed by imitation. Innovations are made by individuals or groups within a given society, and must be followed by an effective job of salesmanship: members of the society must be convinced of the superiority of the new custom over the old. Once innovations become customs in a given society, they are frequently imitated by other societies. Principles and processes of innovation are referred to collectively as *cultural evolution*, and processes of imitation as *cultural diffusion*. The following discussion therefore falls easily into two parts.

Cultural Evolution
and New World Archaeology

Human cultural evolution is similar to biological evolution generally with respect to function: it enables man to compete successfully with other biological organisms, particularly with other men. It differs primarily in process, *i.e.* we encounter modifications of patterned and learned behavior rather than an equivalent of alteration in genes. The basic trends of cultural evolution are clear: increasingly effective technology, widening of resource utilization, discovery of more efficient sources of energy, and larger and internally more complex societies, with development of symbolic systems to make such societies meaningful to their members. Variation in environment may stimulate or retard the tempo of evolution, but the overall direction is indisputable. Viewing cultural evolution as a whole, the tempo generally is an accelerative one as well; as each new plateau has been achieved, subsequent evolution has been faster. The reasons have been noted by a number of anthropologists: the greater the content of a culture, the richer the base for the innovator to work from. Most evolutionists have seen the cause-and-effect chain as leading from technology and energy output, to social and economic institutions, to ideational systems. This position is undoubtedly correct when it refers to gross changes in culture; states cannot evolve before agriculture, but as soon as one analyzes the processes of change within these gross energy levels, it becomes evident that the cause-and-effect relationships are extremely subtle and complex and become circular rather than linear, *i.e.* changes can occur anywhere within a cultural system. A new institution can stimulate development of a new energy level or source as well as vice versa.

Service's evolutionary societal levels are essentially characterized by changes in structure, and these changes are closely correlated with societal size. As a society increases in size it must modify its means of integration in order to function. The processes of societal evolution, therefore, up to and including the level of the ancient state, were essentially demographic ones, particularly the increase of human beings per society. With the Industrial Revolution, a new factor becomes critical; the energy output per individual.

Population growth acts in two ways. First, for a society to function, its members must communicate. Prior to the Industrial Revolution, differences in communication technology varied only slightly. This placed a premium on increase of population density as a precondition to evolution from one societal level to another. Although preindustrial societies also increase in territorial size as they become larger in population, the most significant increase is rather in population density. With more complexly organized states, however, a thoroughly organized communication system based on primitive techniques may permit the organization of unusually large territories; the Inca courier system is an excellent New World example. Population growth also has a more positive effect on societal evolution: it engenders competition, which in turn stimulates experimentation with new cultural forms. This may involve innovations in technology, subsistence, and social structure. Tribes are in a better competitive position than bands; in the same way chiefdoms stand better than tribes, and states better than chiefdoms.

Throughout this book we have periodically raised the questions as to the why and how of precocity and retardation. The fundamental question is not why societal stages were achieved or not achieved in a given culture area; given time societies always evolve to higher levels. The essential question is *why does the tempo vary so strikingly from culture area to culture area?* With this question in mind we will reexamine New World culture history with respect to the evolutionary process.

Bands are closely associated with hunting and gathering, and tribes with agriculture. The major factor that led to societal evolution from band to tribes was essentially the development of agriculture. There are two points of view as to just how the transition occurred. One viewpoint may be referred to as the *hard country* theory. According to this view, hunting and gathering groups residing in a relatively poor environment (in most discussions an arid one), were pressured first into a heavy reliance on wild-plant foods, ultimately to experimentation with methods of artificially increasing the yield. The historic Paiute food-collectors of the Great Basin have been frequently cited as a transitional stage in the shift from hunting and gathering to agriculture. The Paiute exploited wild grasses intensively, frequently irrigated wild-grass plots by canals when drought threatened, and even occasionally extended the habitat of wild grasses by flooding additional land and scattering seed on the moist soil—a primitive technique of planting. The succeeding steps toward a fully agricultural economy involved primarily a botanical process, *i.e.* selection of seed to obtain more productive plants. Evidence from the Tehuacán valley suggests this was precisely what happened.

Other anthropologists and plant geographers have turned the argument around. They argue that the key step is marked by adoption of sedentary residence and that the precarious nature of subsistence in arid environments would inhibit adoption of sedentarianism since the population would not brave the risk of placing all of their ecological eggs in one basket. With respect to Mesoamerica, it is accepted that the first attempts at plant domestication occurred in dry upland regions, but it is felt that agricultural sedentarianism was achieved when primitive crops were diffused to groups who resided in a rich environment and who had already achieved a sedentary mode of residence based on hunting and gathering.[1] The fact that the earliest chiefdoms were found along major rivers of the Gulf Coast Plain has led proponents of this position to the choice of a riparian tropical niche as the probable place of origin. The argument is essentially that such groups would be under less pressure than in arid mountain valleys, and that their achieved riparian sedentarianism would permit them to experiment with agricultural sedentarianism. Sauer has used this argument for the origin both of sedentary agriculture and of the origin of plant domestication in the New World, which he considers a tropical riparian or littoral one.[2]

Archaeological evidence, as we have indicated, seems to point toward multiple origins of plant domestication, and the process probably occurred in a variety of niches. The archaeology of Tehuacán demonstrates the possibility of achieving agricultural sedentarianism in dry upland regions. A serious difficulty of the tropical riparian theory is that no one has ever demonstrated that this niche can support, or ever has supported, a sedentary band ecosystem. The achievement of an agricultural economy explains of itself, with little need for elaboration, the origin of tribal society but cannot alone explain the extraordinary variation in time and space of chiefdoms and states.

[1] Michael D. Coe and Kent V. Flannery, *Early Cultures and Human Ecology in South Coastal Guatemala*, Smithsonian Contribution to Anthropology, vol. 3 (Washington, D.C.: Smithsonian Institution, 1967).

[2] Carl D. Sauer, "Age and Area of American Cultivated Plants," *Actas del XXXIII Congreso Internacional de Americanistas, San Jose, 1958*, I (San Jose, Costa Rica, 1959), pp. 215–229.

Why, once achieved, did agriculture lead to states in Mesoamerica and the Central Andes, to chiefdoms in the Intermediate area, and to tribes in the Southwest? In terms of evolutionary process, why were denser and larger populations achieved in some areas before others? One possible explanation is in purely chronological terms: if agriculture was older in one area than in another, population had a longer period of growth. There is some justification for this position since agriculture is demonstrably earlier in Mesoamerica and the Central Andes; but upon closer inspection, this is obviously not the only factor. Populations remained small—not much over the band level—in the Tehuacán valley until Purrón times (around 2300 B.C.) or, it could be argued, until the Early Ajalpan phase, beginning in 1500 B.C. By 1200 B.C., chiefdoms were well established in neighboring areas, and, by A.D. 1, states were too. Agriculture of the same level of efficiency and population density of comparable level were present in the Intermediate area by 1000 B.C., but chiefdoms did not appear until a few centuries B.C. and did not become common until after A.D. 500; the state level was never achieved. A comparable agricultural economy was present in portions of the Amazon Basin between 1000 and 500 B.C., yet most groups remained tribally organized as late as Contact. In the Southwest and the Southern Andes, sedentary village life appeared as early as 300 B.C., but society in both areas remained tribal throughout. If these data are arranged on a graph, (our chronological chart can be easily used as a graph), it becomes obvious that factors other than that of chronology are involved.

One obvious inhibiting factor is seen in the total demographic potential of a region. The Southern Andes and the Southwest were both arid regions with scanty resources. The total population of farmers in the Southwest at time of Contact did not exceed 60,000; overall density is estimated at .11 per sq km. Neither states nor chiefdoms can function in such a demographic setting.

Another clue lies in the agricultural system itself. One type of New World agriculture, the tropical forest pattern of Amazonia, involves a combination of starchy roots with wild protein foods. The caloric yield and demographic potential of manioc is very high, even with extensive agricultural practices, but as long as it was linked to dependence on wild protein foods its demographic potential could not be realized.

The major factor, however, seems to relate to the reaction of farmers to population pressure. One striking geographical fact linking both chiefdoms and states in the New World is their close correlation with James's complex mountain type, an environment characterized by intense microgeographic zoning. This type of environment has two major ecological effects; it stimulates evolution of a great variety of specialized ecosystems, each adapted to a particular niche, and imposes tight limits on their geographic expansion. Variation occurs not only in the species and races of crops, but in cultivation techniques and cycles. Although we defined two basic ecosystems for Mesoamerica—tropical lowland and arid highland—in fact, each type embraced a great number of spatially restricted microadaptations. Even within a single mountain valley there are striking variations in type of agricultural land, so that a single topographic unit requires a variety of adaptive responses. In complex mountain environments there is also a considerable variation in other types of resources as well.

Carneiro [3] has referred to the critical characteristic of the complex mountain environment as a *circumscribed environment* and has contrasted it with the Amazon Basin, which he refers to as an *open environment*. The terminology is in reference to differences in response by cultivators to population pressure.

Extensive cultivation, with few exceptions, is a more economic system in terms of work–production ratios (because of the striking decline of yield between new fields and those successively cultivated) than is intensive cultivation. The usual response to population pressure is, therefore, fission or local migration rather than intensification or land use. Villages remain small in size and stable in population as the product of a continuous process of the splitting off of lineages or families to found new settlements in nearby areas.

In an open environment fissioning can occur almost indefinitely. A consequence of this is that while we may see a continuous expansion of range of cultivation, the rate of increase of population density is extremely slow. In circumscribed environments this type of response can occur only in the pioneer stage of occupation. The restricted spatial possibilities presented by specialized ecosystems and topographical barriers to population movement force the cultivator early in the history of the region to shift to more intensive agricultural practices. In later phases of adaptation local groups may specialize in particular crops or in extraction and processing of other resources. The overall result is a much faster rate of increase in population density. Within any given topographic unit there are considerable variations in crop productivity and hence in population density. For these reasons, groups located in favorable niches enjoy a competitive advantage and ultimately are able politically to dominate groups located in less favorable areas. The social response to these ecological processes is the chiefdom, a ranked society that has as its major function the collection and redistribution of surplus produced by economically specialized local communities. The social structure of a chiefdom, once established, may also function to increase the demographic potential of a local area in a variety of ways, which is another illustration of the circular aspect of causation in cultural systems. Chiefs may organize and stimulate further patterns of local specialization, organize labor for construction of terraces, or organize the population militarily and exact tribute from neighboring chiefdoms or tribes. The great variability in environmental characteristics and variable resources of neighboring areas acts as a stimulus, first to trade, ultimately to political expansion. Of these activities, perhaps the most significant is the development of irrigation, since it provides the chief with a new dimension of power: control of water.

This brings us to the final phase of our discussion of cultural evolution in the New World, the evolution of states. We wish first to reiterate a point made several times in the course of our discussion of cultural evolution: we are treating of precocity, not absolute factors or limits of cultural evolution. The major factors that led to a precocious evolution of states in both Mesoamerica and the Central Andes was the development of what Wittfogel has

---

[3] Robert L. Carneiro, "Slash and Burn Cultivation among the Kuikuru and Its Implications for Cultural Development in the Amazon Basin, Caracas. Anthropologica, no. 10 (1961).

called hydraulic agriculture—based on water works, their construction, maintenance, and operation.[4] The effects of irrigation agriculture are of two kinds, internal and external. The major difference between chief and king is the nature of their power, its degree of absoluteness, and the character of the economic base. Investment of the control of water in the hands of a chief was probably the most significant factor in the transformation of his status to that of king. Furthermore, irrigation agriculture is enormously more productive than any other system of cultivation and hence has greater demographic potential as well. This means larger and denser populations. Such a demographic setting facilitated the operation and functioning of the state. A further aspect of the integrative effects of hydraulic agriculture is that they provided the necessary economic base for evolution of urban centers. Finally, water resources are always limited in quantity and restricted in distribution. Hydraulic chiefdoms and states would enjoy a highly advantageous competitive position with respect to nonhydraulic polities. All the empires of Mesoamerica were centered in the Central Plateau, where hydraulic agriculture reached its maximal development.

In a comparison of culture histories of the Central Andes and Mesoamerica, the ecological processes noted may explain many differences in precocity of stages between the two areas as well as among various subareas within the culture areas. Archaeologists in both areas have noted that smaller mountain valleys, desert oases, and coastal plains were more precocious in the earlier stages of cultural evolution, and that centers of development shifted to larger ecozones in the later phases. This pattern undoubtedly relates to variations in rates of population growth. Furthermore, Andean ecozones are smaller generally than those in Mesoamerica; the more rapid evolution of chiefdoms in the Central Andes may relate to this fact. Also related to this Andean precocity may be the greater stimulus towards evolution of more intensive patterns of land use found in both the desert oases and mountain valleys. The possibly very early evolution of a small state in the Casma Valley was noted. It is tempting to relate this to the far more critical role of hydraulic agriculture in the coastal Central Andean province than in Mesoamerica. On the other hand, the first truly large states and urban centers are demonstrably older in Mesoamerica. The small size and wide spacing of Central Andean population clusters would act as a powerful inhibitory factor with respect to this level of societal evolution; however, the very same inhibitory factor, in the final phase of Central Andean history, acted as a powerful stimulus towards a more highly centralized political structure. The Inca were more highly organized than the Aztec because they had to be. The greater topographic fragmentation would demand a tighter administrative organization for the state to function. This is another example of the subtle and circular way in which environment and culture interact.

With respect to ecological processes, Mesoamerica differs from the Central Andes in several other important respects. First, a sizable part of the region is tropical lowland where integral swidden was the most intensive type of agriculture practicable. Societal evolution in such areas lacked the socioeconomic system we have referred to as urban. Second, much of the upland

---

[4] Karl A. Wittfogel, *Oriental Despotism. A Comparative Study of Total Power* (New Haven: Yale University Press, 1957), p. 556.

portions of Mesoamerica can support relatively dense populations with extensive practice of cultivation. This retarded the evolution of intensive agriculture during most of the Formative Period; the evolution of chiefdoms took place in a setting of extensive agriculture. Swidden is most productive in a tropical lowland riparian niche, and the largest Formative chiefdoms were found in precisely this type of environment. Major population and political centers did not appear in the uplands of Mesoamerica until the end of the Formative and the development of intensive agriculture. Finally, although both regions are geographically complex, this complexity is most marked in Mesoamerica; as a consequence, trade was here a much more vital factor in the societal evolution. The effort to control this trade provided one of the most powerful stimuli towards the expansion of chiefdoms and particularly of states. Trading institutions such as merchant guilds and markets were more highly developed.

Diffusion
and New World Archaeology

Having defined evolutionary processes involved in societal evolution in the New World, we are now in a better position to evaluate the significance of diffusion as a process of New World culture history

A major problem in archaeological research generally is in establishing guidelines to determine whether cultural similarities were the product of diffusion or of parallel evolutionary processes. There is a wide spectrum of opinion about what constitutes evidence of diffusion and about the nature of laws of probability with respect to duplication of basic customs, or, more particularly, of specific styles of customs. Wilhelm Schmidt, the German ethnologist, tried to establish such guidelines some time ago;[5] he referred to them as *criteria* and listed three: *quantity, quality,* and *opportunity.* By quantity he meant the sheer number of traits shared by two cultures. This is not a simple criterion to apply: if one uses very generalized customs like polygynous marriage, belief in ghosts, or use of stone projectile points, then correspondences of traits running into hundreds could be compiled for the hundreds of cultures that obviously have had no specific historical contact.

Schmidt's criterion of *quality* is somewhat more manageable; here he was referring to something akin to what archaeologists refer to as *stylistic complexes* or *traditions,* particularly in their more complex manifestations. Here again, however, we run into methodological problems. Just how internally complex must a style tradition be before we can postulate diffusion? Many archaeologists have postulated direct contacts between Mesoamerica and the Central Andes simply on the basis of style modes or individual elements of style, such as a vessel form. Here, perhaps, Schmidt's third criterion, that of *opportunity,* may provide the key principle. By opportunity Schmidt meant the conjunction of the two subcriteria of time and space. Two cultures must be contemporary and close enough in space to establish contact. Just how close they must be depends on the level of transportation and communication

⁵ Wilhelm Schmidt, *The Culture Historical Method of Ethnology: The Scientific Approach to the Racial Question,* trans. S. A. Sieber (New York: Fortuny's, 1939).

technology. The closer two groups are, the greater the probability of contact and borrowing; the farther apart they are, the greater the probability of independent invention. Style modes are particularly poor criteria to use as bases for assuming secondary diffusion: they are not internally complex enough to qualify as criteria of quality and they recur repeatedly in culture history as independent events; however, they are undoubtedly useful in tracing primary diffusion. In short, entirely different criteria should be used in evaluating possible evidence of diffusion over great distances as against short ones, and reliable evidence of secondary diffusion must be based on similarities in complex style traditions and not on similarities in style modes.

In discussions of the mechanism of diffusion, archaeologists frequently fail to observe distinctions between technological levels, and even more frequently between social levels. All American Indian cultures were characterized by extremely primitive transportation and communication technology; diffusion generally played a much less significant role in their culture history than it has in this age of mass communication. Within the societal levels found among the native population, diffusion would also vary considerably in its intensity and nature, and in the mechanism of transmission.

Parochialism operates in all societal levels to inhibit external diffusion. Innovations are more likely to diffuse within the society of the inventor than without. As one moves along the continuum from band to state, this ingroup becomes larger in population and, particularly on the state level, in territory. The consequence is a speedup in the tempo of diffusion and an increase in its demographic and geographic range.

Competition is a major stimulus not only to innovation but also to diffusion; it operates on all societal levels, especially where a new custom provides a group with an advantage in control and use of resources. Much of the effect of competition is indirect, particularly with respect to social innovations. Tribes cannot permanently survive in a social setting of chiefdoms, nor can chiefdoms in a setting of states.

The diffusion of even social "inventions," however, may be more direct. Tribal warfare frequently involves wholesale adoption of conquered groups, providing an additional mechanism of diffusion. The direct effects of competition are particularly characteristic of chiefdoms and states, since conquest is followed by regularized economic exploitation, and the opportunities for diffusion become enormously expanded. Furthermore, a new factor is involved that considerably accelerates the pace of diffusion. This is the structural principle of rank, or differential prestige. Wholly aside from the coercive aspect of diffusion in such a social setting, chiefdom or kingly lineages and political centers operate as fashion producers and centers of innovation. Ideas accepted by prestigious leaders and communities are apt to find rapid acceptance. Imitation may involve a great variety of customs, including even highly specific stylistic variations of customs that have no survival value. This factor may also operate with respect to diffusion between independent polities, since they always vary in size, wealth, and population—and, hence, in prestige.

Trade is a powerful mechanism for diffusion, particularly of the technological features of culture, but on the higher levels of societal complexity it may involve much more. Natural resources are always unevenly distributed, and all societies engage in some trade, which varies enormously in significance from level to level. Bands produce few surpluses, their technological needs are simple, and trade is a minor factor in diffusion. As one proceeds to higher levels of social integration, specialization becomes more intense, surpluses are larger, and trade is an increasingly more significant factor in cultural diffusion. On the state level, a market and professional merchants may add another dimension to the picture. Craft guilds may even migrate to new markets as the political fortunes of centers wax and wane.

This brings us to the general subject of migration. Recently in New World archaeology there has been a strong revival of interest in migration as a mechanism of cultural diffusion. This trend is unfortunate and it is doubtful whether migrations—at least large-scale movements of population over great distances—have been common enough in human history to play a major role in cultural diffusion. Hunters, gatherers, and farmers (whether tribesmen or peasants) achieve very close and delicately balanced adaptations to their environments—adaptations that are often combined with strong emotional ties to the land. As a consequence, such groups move only under unusually compelling pressures. The linguistic picture of the New World argues strongly against massive population movement. Historic distributions of the taxonomic levels correlate strikingly with cultural traditions of great chronological depth.

A much more common mechanism of cultural diffusion is *fission*. Fission is particularly characteristic of tropical swidden cultivators but occurs among most cultivators residing in areas of abundant land; it is also a common process among hunters and gatherers as bands outgrow their territories. By the process of fission, gradual expansion of a cultural system over a huge territory may ultimately occur. Among the more complexly structured chiefdoms, and more particularly among states, long-distance migration of small, specialized groups, such as priests, warriors, colonists, craftsmen, and merchants are common events and one of the major mechanisms of diffusion.

There is little doubt that primary diffusion played a vital role in the formation of the regional traditions referred to as culture areas. In the discussion of the history of culture areas, we noted a variety of examples of diffusion, from ceramic modes to religious systems. However, the nature of diffusion varies strikingly; it is primarily correlated with social level. Although the process of diffusion and the kinds of things diffused differ from level to level, the major break seems to occur between tribes and chiefdoms.

The kinds of things that seem to diffuse widely in a band social setting are basic tools, such as a spear-thrower, or such small stylistic modes as fluted points. What does *not* diffuse widely are complex style traditions [6] or whole cultural traditions. The latter may be distributed over huge territories, as in the case of the Big-Game Hunting tradition, but this is not really so much the product of migration and diffusion as of fission and parallel adaptive evolution. Much of the diffusion of minor stylistic modes and basic ideas within a band societal context occurs between neighboring groups and is probably the product of regularized exogamous and ceremonial relationships. Bands that have similar ecosystems are more apt to intermarry, share religious

---

[6] The only kind of direct evidence of style that archaeologists have is technological. Hunting and gathering groups have such a simple level of technology that complex technological style traditions do not exist in any case. The reference here is to styles of religion or social structure.

ceremonies, and consequently exchange customs. Much of the phylum level of linguistic differentiation was probably the product of this preferential interaction.

Tribal diffusion seems to be similar to band diffusion in many ways. A number of archaeologists would place greater emphasis on migration at this level; Evans [7] has explained much of the history of the Tropical Forest pattern in this way. The sharp local divergence that he notes from site to site would rather suggest fission as the process, in this case with a strikingly linear geographical pattern—the product of the peculiar Tropical Forest ecosystem. Migrations do occur among tribes, as in the case of the Anasazi penetration of the Gila River Basin, but only as the product of ecological disasters. Generally, diffusion among both bands and tribes occurs between neighboring groups and, as we noted, involves primarily style modes and basic customs.

On the chiefdom and state levels, diffusion tends to take on a strikingly different character. Diffusion of stylistic modes and basic customs continues to occur. In fact, this process is accelerated and intensified as the product of denser population and organized trade. Added to this type of diffusion is that of internally complex stylistic traditions or whole cultural traditions. Among chiefdoms, the two major mechanisms of this kind of diffusion are migration and, more importantly, organized trade. Known cases of migration seem all to be the product of forcible expulsion of smaller chiefdoms by larger ones. Survival of these isolated groups probably depended on their having migrated to areas occupied by tribes, where the more highly integrated structure of the intruders enabled them to survive. A striking example of this type of diffusion is seen in the case of the Middle Mississippian expansion. The diffusion of the Olmec and Chavín style complexes, however, was probably the product of trade organized by the large chiefdoms, a trade stimulated by the heterogeneity of the complex mountain environment.

Among states, political incorporation takes on added significance as a mechanism of diffusion, as does trade. Generally speaking, the patterns of diffusion among states seem essentially an intensification of the diffusion found among chiefdoms, except that migration of specialized groups is a more significant factor. As a consequence, the diffusion of complex style traditions and of whole cultural traditions is characteristic of states.

The subject of secondary diffusion is highly controversial. All archaeologists accept the idea that secondary diffusion has occurred in New World culture history and that the distribution of basic technological traits or complexes such as pottery, agriculture, loom weaving, and metallurgy can be understood only as the product of secondary diffusion. Archaeologists are divided on the question of whether these traits and complexes had single or multiple origins. The data strongly suggest multiple origins for such items as pottery, agriculture, and loom weaving; metallurgy probably had a single Central Andean origin. One interpretation of the origin and diffusion of New World agriculture was presented in Chapter Four. Ceramics originated, or at least diffused, from a minimum of five separate centers: the Eastern Woodlands (where it may have had two separate histories); Mesoamerica;

----

[7] Clifford Evans, "Lowland South America," in Jesse Jennings and Edward Norbeck, eds., *Prehistoric Man in the New World* (Chicago: The University of Chicago Press, 1963), pp. 419–450.

the Caribbean Coast of Colombia; the Pacific Coast of Ecuador; and the Pacific Coast of Alaska. The last two centers, and one of the woodland centers (that of the Northern tradition), have been ascribed to an Asiatic origin. Much secondary diffusion of basic technological traits was probably the product of gradual diffusion between neighboring groups.

The major controversy is over the possible direct diffusion of style modes, style complexes, and whole cultural traditions between culture areas located at a considerable distance from each other. In the case of style modes, for example, a great number of similarities in ceramic modes have been noted between the Central Andes and Mesoamerica; these occur in tripod supports, pedestal-base vessels, stirrup-spout jars, long-necked bottles, tecomates, flat-bottom-flaresided bowls, composite silhouette bowls, negative painting, polychrome painting, rocker stamping, and dentate stamping, to name a few; the list is almost endless. Moving away from ceramics, both areas shared such religious symbols as felines, dual gods, serpents, and raptorial birds.

With respect to culture areas that border each other, the mechanism of diffusion differed in no way from those described for primary diffusion. It is extremely doubtful whether intermittent, accidental migrations or visits by small groups have ever played a significant role in cultural diffusion. Cultures are too conservative, too resistant to change. The extraordinary persistence of native cultures, even in a social setting of continuous contact and organized exploitation by highly advanced modern nations, is dramatic testimony of the capacity of even the simplest cultures to resist change. The only possible mechanisms for direct secondary diffusion over considerable distance are regularized trade and substantial migrations. Arguing strongly against such migrations is the lack of evidence of diffusion of style complexes or whole cultural traditions. Even in the Ecuadorean case cited (the Esmeraldas chiefdoms), the resemblances are really quantitative and consist of a great number of ceramic style modes. Trade is a conceivable mechanism of secondary diffusion, but native transportation was incapable of sustained, regularized trade over such long distances; furthermore, it is difficult to conceive of an incentive for such trade; finally, no trade objects have been reported for either of the two areas. Much of the similarity of basic traits and style modes between the Central Andes and Mesoamerica is undoubtedly the product of parallel evolution, with some diffusion from group to group through the Intermediate area.

One particularly revealing fact about recent claims of long-range migrations within the Americas is that most of the adduced cases involve relatively early phases of ceramic sequences and groups that were tribally organized or were organized maximally into small chiefdoms. One would expect that the pace of diffusion would increase during the later phases within the social setting of large chiefdoms and states. Again, the answer relates to the nature of stylistic evolution. Most of the arguments in favor of diffusion are based on similarities in ceramic modes found in ceramic complexes characterized by plastic design or by very simple painting design. Plastic design always seems to precede painted design in local ceramic histories and has a much more restricted range of possibilities in variety of motif. Duplication of design is therefore not surprising, nor is it a reliable indicator of secondary diffusion.

These arguments apply with even greater force to any postulated trans-Pacific diffusion. In this case, the only conceivable mechanism could be sporadic, fortuitous migrations of small groups. That such contacts could have had much effect on New World culture history is incredible. Successful diffusion demands the sustained, periodic communication of the types already described, and none of the evidence presented involves more than stylistic modes and basic cultural traits. Even the postulated Valdivia-Jomon resemblances are essentially quantitative and consist of ceramic modes, again primarily comprising techniques and motifs of plastic design rather than style traditions.

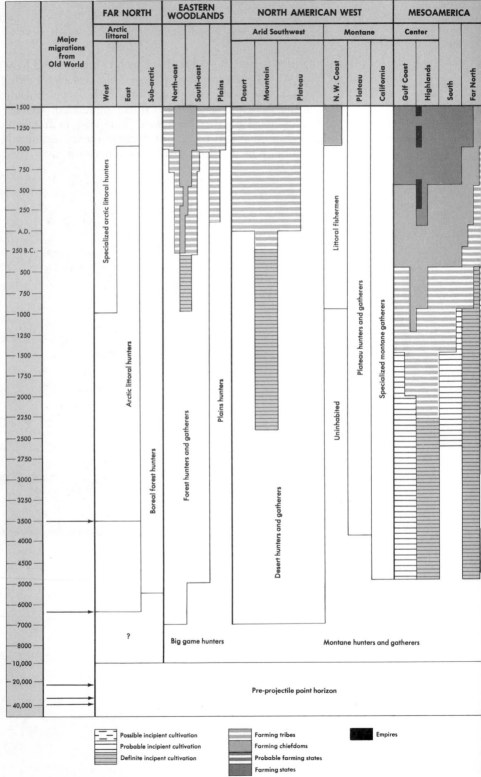

Figure 1. Period and stage in New World culture history.

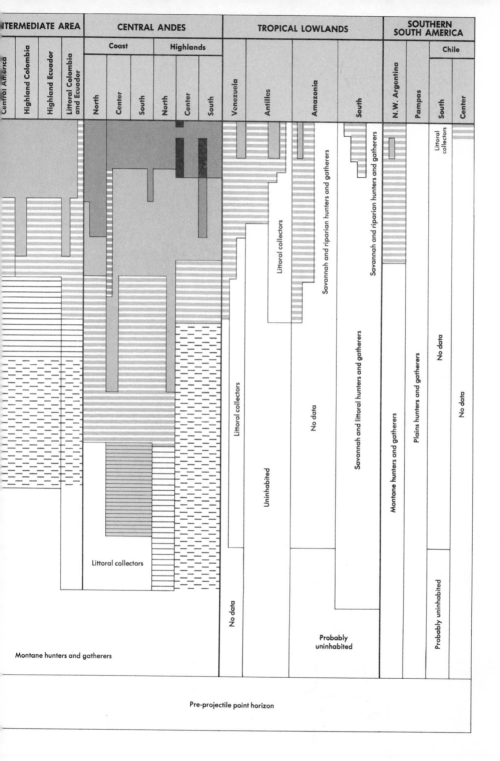

INTERMEDIATE AREA				CENTRAL ANDES						TROPICAL LOWLANDS				SOUTHERN SOUTH AMERICA			
				Coast			Highlands									Chile	
Central America	Highland Colombia	Highland Ecuador	Littoral Colombia and Ecuador	North	Center	South	North	Center	South	Venezuela	Antilles	Amazonia	South	N.W. Argentina	Pampas	South	Center

Montane hunters and gatherers

Littoral collectors

Littoral collectors

Littoral collectors

Savannah and riparian hunters and gatherers

Savannah and riparian hunters and gatherers

Savannah and littoral hunters and gatherers

No data

Uninhabited

Montane hunters and gatherers

Plains hunters and gatherers

Littoral collectors

No data

No data

Probably uninhabited

No data

Probably uninhabited

Pre-projectile point horizon

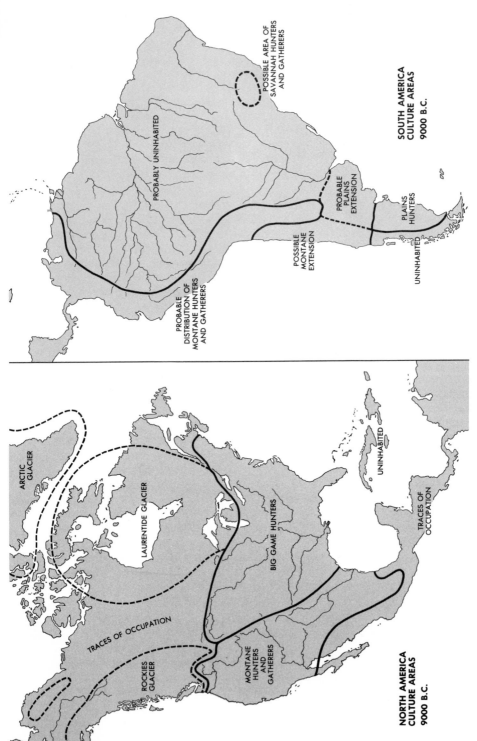

Figure 2. New World culture areas, North and South America, 9000 B.C.

**NORTH AMERICA
CULTURE AREAS
9000 B.C.**

ARCTIC GLACIER

LAURENTIDE GLACIER

ROCKIES GLACIER

TRACES OF OCCUPATION

TRACES OF OCCUPATION

BIG GAME HUNTERS

MONTANE HUNTERS AND GATHERERS

UNINHABITED

**SOUTH AMERICA
CULTURE AREAS
9000 B.C.**

PROBABLY UNINHABITED

POSSIBLE AREA OF SAVANNAH HUNTERS AND GATHERERS

PROBABLE DISTRIBUTION OF MONTANE HUNTERS AND GATHERERS

POSSIBLE MONTANE EXTENSION

PROBABLE PLAINS EXTENSION

PLAINS HUNTERS

UNINHABITED

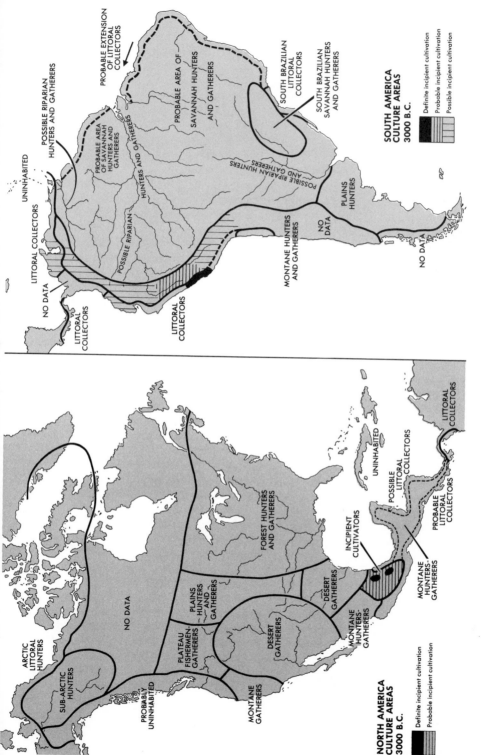

NORTH AMERICA
CULTURE AREAS
3000 B.C.

■ Definite incipient cultivation
▥ Probable incipient cultivation

ARCTIC LITTORAL HUNTERS

SUB-ARCTIC HUNTERS

PROBABLY UNINHABITED

NO DATA

PLATEAU FISHERMEN-GATHERERS

PLAINS HUNTERS AND GATHERERS

FOREST HUNTERS AND GATHERERS

DESERT GATHERERS

MONTANE GATHERERS

MONTANE HUNTERS-GATHERERS

DESERT GATHERERS

MONTANE HUNTERS-GATHERERS

INCIPIENT CULTIVATORS

UNINHABITED

POSSIBLE LITTORAL COLLECTORS

PROBABLE LITTORAL COLLECTORS

LITTORAL COLLECTORS

SOUTH AMERICA
CULTURE AREAS
3000 B.C.

■ Definite incipient cultivation
▥ Probable incipient cultivation
▤ Possible incipient cultivation

PROBABLE EXTENSION OF LITTORAL COLLECTORS

POSSIBLE RIPARIAN HUNTERS AND GATHERERS

UNINHABITED

NO DATA

LITTORAL COLLECTORS

LITTORAL COLLECTORS

LITTORAL COLLECTORS

POSSIBLE RIPARIAN HUNTERS AND GATHERERS

PROBABLE AREA OF SAVANNAH HUNTERS AND GATHERERS

PROBABLE AREA OF SAVANNAH HUNTERS AND GATHERERS

SOUTH BRAZILIAN LITTORAL COLLECTORS

SOUTH BRAZILIAN SAVANNAH HUNTERS AND GATHERERS

POSSIBLE RIPARIAN HUNTERS AND GATHERERS

MONTANE HUNTERS AND GATHERERS

NO DATA

PLAINS HUNTERS

NO DATA

Figure 3. New World culture areas, North and South America, 3000 B.C.

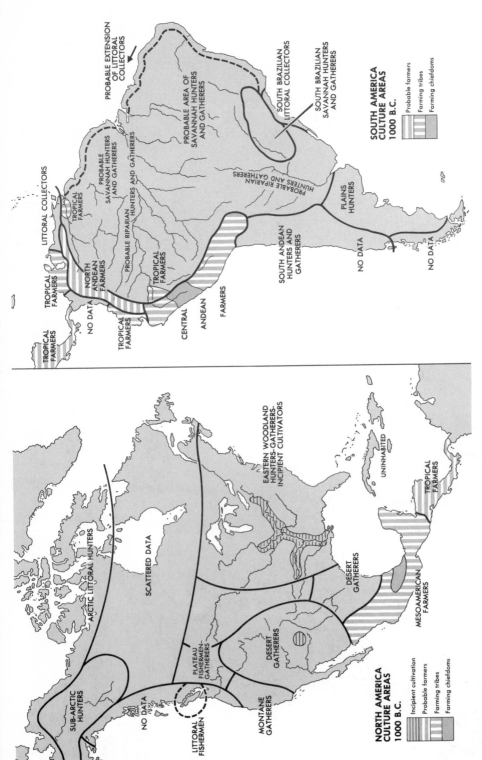

Figure 4. *New World culture areas, North and South America, 1000 B.C.*

NORTH AMERICA CULTURE AREAS 1000 B.C.

Incipient cultivation
Probable farmers
Farming tribes
Farming chiefdoms

ARCTIC LITTORAL HUNTERS

SUB-ARCTIC HUNTERS

SCATTERED DATA

NO DATA

LITTORAL FISHERMEN

PLATEAU FISHERMEN-GATHERERS

MONTANE GATHERERS

DESERT GATHERERS

DESERT GATHERERS

EASTERN WOODLAND HUNTERS-GATHERERS-INCIPIENT CULTIVATORS

UNINHABITED

TROPICAL FARMERS

MESOAMERICAN FARMERS

SOUTH AMERICA CULTURE AREAS 1000 B.C.

Probable farmers
Farming tribes
Farming chiefdoms

LITTORAL COLLECTORS

TROPICAL FARMERS

NO DATA

TROPICAL FARMERS

NORTH ANDEAN FARMERS

TROPICAL FARMERS

CENTRAL ANDEAN FARMERS

PROBABLE EXTENSION OF LITTORAL COLLECTORS

PROBABLE SAVANNAH HUNTERS AND GATHERERS

PROBABLE RIPARIAN HUNTERS AND GATHERERS

TROPICAL FARMERS

PROBABLE AREA OF SAVANNAH HUNTERS AND GATHERERS

PROBABLE RIPARIAN HUNTERS AND GATHERERS

SOUTH BRAZILIAN LITTORAL COLLECTORS

SOUTH BRAZILIAN SAVANNAH HUNTERS AND GATHERERS

SOUTH ANDEAN HUNTERS AND GATHERERS

PLAINS HUNTERS

NO DATA

NO DATA

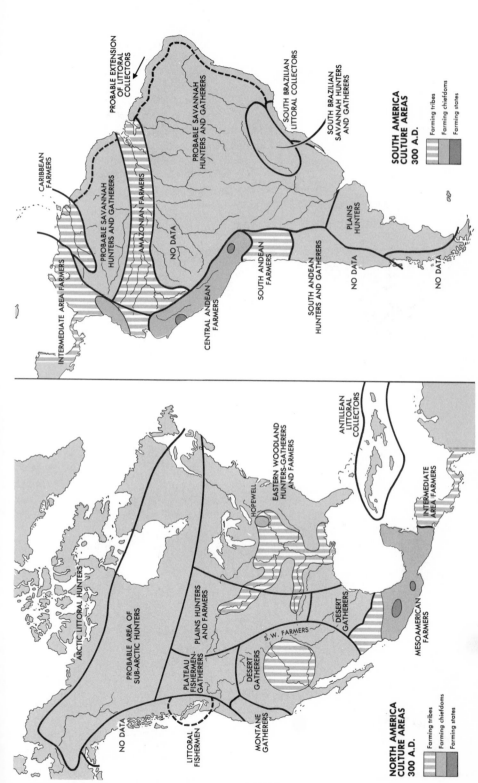

Figure 5. New World culture areas, North and South America, 300 A.D.

NORTH AMERICA CULTURE AREAS 300 A.D.

Farming tribes
Farming chiefdoms
Farming states

NO DATA

ARCTIC LITTORAL HUNTERS

PROBABLE AREA OF SUB-ARCTIC HUNTERS

LITTORAL FISHERMEN

PLATEAU FISHERMEN-GATHERERS

PLAINS HUNTERS AND FARMERS

HOPEWELL

EASTERN WOODLAND HUNTERS-GATHERERS AND FARMERS

ANTILLEAN LITTORAL COLLECTORS

S.W. FARMERS

DESERT GATHERERS

MONTANE GATHERERS

DESERT GATHERERS

MESOAMERICAN FARMERS

INTERMEDIATE AREA FARMERS

SOUTH AMERICA CULTURE AREAS 300 A.D.

Farming tribes
Farming chiefdoms
Farming states

PROBABLE EXTENSION OF LITTORAL COLLECTORS

CARIBBEAN FARMERS

INTERMEDIATE AREA FARMERS

PROBABLE SAVANNAH HUNTERS AND GATHERERS

AMAZONIAN FARMERS

NO DATA

PROBABLE SAVANNAH HUNTERS AND GATHERERS

SOUTH BRAZILIAN LITTORAL COLLECTORS

SOUTH BRAZILIAN SAVANNAH HUNTERS AND GATHERERS

CENTRAL ANDEAN FARMERS

SOUTH ANDEAN FARMERS

SOUTH ANDEAN HUNTERS AND GATHERERS

PLAINS HUNTERS

NO DATA

NO DATA

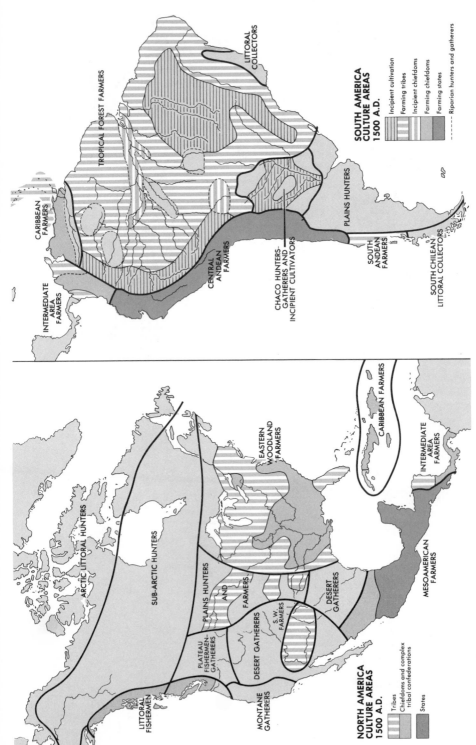

NORTH AMERICA
CULTURE AREAS
1500 A.D.

Tribes
Chiefdoms and complex
tribal confederations
States

ARCTIC LITTORAL HUNTERS

SUB-ARCTIC HUNTERS

EASTERN
WOODLAND
FARMERS

LITTORAL FISHERMEN

PLATEAU FISHERMEN-GATHERERS

PLAINS HUNTERS
AND
FARMERS

S.W. FARMERS

DESERT GATHERERS

DESERT GATHERERS

MONTANE GATHERERS

MESOAMERICAN FARMERS

CARIBBEAN FARMERS

INTERMEDIATE AREA FARMERS

SOUTH AMERICA
CULTURE AREAS
1500 A.D.

Incipient cultivation
Farming tribes
Incipient chiefdoms
Farming chiefdoms
Farming states
Riparian hunters and gatherers

CARIBBEAN FARMERS

INTERMEDIATE AREA FARMERS

TROPICAL FOREST FARMERS

LITTORAL COLLECTORS

CENTRAL ANDEAN FARMERS

CHACO HUNTERS-GATHERERS AND INCIPIENT CULTIVATORS

PLAINS HUNTERS

SOUTH ANDEAN FARMERS

SOUTH CHILEAN LITTORAL COLLECTORS

Figure 6. New World culture areas, North and South America, 1500 A.D.

Index